Income Redistribution and the Social Security Program

Research in Business Economics and Public Policy, No. 12

Fred Bateman, Series Editor

Chairman and Professor
Business Economics and Public Policy
Indiana University

Other Titles in This Series

No. 5	*The Dominant Firm: A Study of Market Power*	Alice Patricia White
No. 7	*Inventory and Production Decisions*	Mansfield W. Williams
No. 8	*Multinational Banks: Their Identities and Determinants*	Kang Rae Cho
No. 9	*The Effect of Research and Development on U.S. Market Structure*	Edward M. Scahill
No. 10	*The Financing of Technological Change*	Lorne N. Switzer
No. 11	*Labor Force Participation of Black and White Youth*	Donald R. Williams

Income Redistribution and the Social Security Program

by
Nancy Wolff

Ann Arbor / London

Produced and distributed by
UMI Research Press
an imprint of
University Microfilms, Inc.
Ann Arbor, Michigan 48106

Library of Congress Cataloging in Publication Data

Wolff, Nancy, 1955-
Income redistribution and the Social Security program.

(Research in business economics and public policy ; no. 12)
Revision of thesis (Ph.D.)—Iowa State University, 1984.
Bibliography: p.
Includes index.
1. Old age pensions—United States. 2. Social security—United States. 3. Income distribution—United States. 4. Retirement income—United States. 5. Distributive justice. I. Title. II. Series.
HD7105.35.U6W65 1987 368.4'3'00973 87-10791
ISBN 0-8357-1807-7 (alk. paper)

Contents

Acknowledgments

I wish to record my thanks and gratitude to the many people who generously gave their time and knowledge to assist me in writing this book. I would especially like to thank Charles W. Meyer, who has worked with me on this study from its inception. His advice, constructive criticism, and suggestions have greatly improved the final product. I am also indebted to Dennis Starleaf, Dudley Luckett, J. Peter Mattila, and Fred Lorenz for their helpful suggestions on preliminary versions of the book. For technical assistance, I would like to express my personal appreciation to numerous persons: to Mark Movic of Banker's Life for his actuarial expertise and many suggestions on the annuity formulas; to Bud Meader of the Statistical and Numerical Analysis Lab at Iowa State University for his personal approval of computation work to be conducted by employees of the Stat Lab; to Leann Crowder of the Statistical and Numerical Analysis Lab for her superior computer programming skills and conscientiousness; to Fred Hulting of the Statistical and Numerical Analysis Lab for his programming assistance and diligence; and to Diana McLaughlin for her excellent typing and proofreading skills.

Friends and family assisted in important ways. Dee Stupp-Hurst offered me hospitality, friendship, and humor on my research visits. Extra special thanks to my husband, Keith Heimforth, for his insight, support, and encouragement.

Introduction

For over five decades, the Social Security program[1] has grown in scope, worker coverage, budgetary significance, and, until quite recently, popularity. However, the federal Old-Age, Survivors, Disability, and Health Insurance (OASDHI) program has entered a new phase in its long, convoluted history—a phase marked by public confusion, critical debate, budgetary insolvency, and controversy. This book investigates one cause of the controversy, the income redistribution objective of the program. The old-age insurance portion of the Social Security program has two primary objectives: 1) to insure retirees against economic risk over an uncertain retirement period when potential earnings are low or zero, and 2) to redistribute income within an age cohort and across generations. The former objective alters the pattern of income receipts across the individual's life cycle, whereas the latter alters the distribution of lifetime income within an age cohort and across generations. Over time, policymakers have shifted the emphasis of the program away from traditional insurance principles, or "individual equity," toward a distribution of benefits based on the presumptive needs of retired persons and their dependents, or "social adequacy."

The primary, although not exclusive, emphasis of the program has become an attempt to extend a minimum standard of income security to all retired persons in pursuance of social justice. The apparent dual nature of the program was not problematic until recently because taxes were kept at acceptable levels, covered retirees were generally net gainers, and, to a lesser extent, the program was conveniently cast in a traditional insurance-like framework. The first generation of OAI beneficiaries received exorbitant rates of return on prior OAI contributions owing to the fact that they had few years of coverage in the program and a relatively long benefit collection period. Subsequent generations have benefited from the relative immaturity of the program, which made possible extremely low tax rates and frequent increases in benefit levels. As the system matures, meaning the contribution period eclipses the entire work history, the size of the intergenerational transfer will diminish.[2] In addition, the probability of being a net loser will increase, drawing further attention to the cause of the potential loser-gainer scenario—the redistribution objective.

The waning of the potential gains from the Social Security program has led many Americans to question whether the system is "fair." Fairness, in this context, refers to whether retirement benefits are closely tied to payroll tax contributions. That is, do workers with identical (or similar) earnings records receive the same retirement benefit amounts? The answer to this question is by no means unequivocal; rather, it depends on a whole host of interrelated worker-specific factors (e.g., age at retirement, marital status, postretirement earnings levels, and year of retirement). Consequently, the current system may provide retirees with more benefits than are warranted by their contributions to the system. The existence of potential inequities under Social Security, however, should not be surprising in light of the dual nature of the program. Recall that the social adequacy objective, in essence, mandates income redistribution within and across cohorts and, as a consequence, it conflicts with the individual equity objective. In recent years, the inherent conflict between adequacy and equity objectives has been heightened, focusing greater public attention on program inequities.

Issues of inequities have been raised by younger workers, single workers, women, especially married women who work outside the home, and working persons aged 62 to 72 (70 after 1982) (Campbell, 1977a and 1977b). First, the inequity issue between young and older workers arises because earlier cohorts receive, on average, substantially higher rates of return on their payroll contributions than later cohorts.[3] Historically, rates of return on combined payroll taxes have fallen. For example, the real rate of return on combined payroll taxes has decreased from an estimated 20 percent to approximately 9 percent for cohorts born between 1875 and 1910 (Moffit, 1982). Projected rates of return for workers entering the labor force between 1960 and 2000 are considerably lower, ranging from −1.5 to 4 percent depending on the study and the underlying demographic and economic performance assumptions.[4] The historical disparity in rates of return on payroll contributions has caused many young workers to lose confidence in the program. They question both the fairness and appropriateness of employing an "early bird gets the worm" principle in determining the rate of return on payroll contributions.

Second, the provision of noncontributory spousal dependents benefits has produced serious inequities between 1) married and single workers, 2) one- and two-earner couples, and 3) women divorced after less than 10 years of marriage and other divorced women. The inequity between single and married workers arises because single workers, like married workers, are compulsorily affiliated to a family-based Social Security program; they pay the same payroll tax contributions, based on occupational income, but the married workers, in principle, receive a more comprehensive package of benefits—insured worker *plus* noncontributory spousal benefits (equal to 50 percent of the insured worker benefit). Consequently, a dollar's worth of contributions made by a married worker (potentially) generates 50 percent more benefits than the same dollar's worth of contributions made by a single worker.

Similarly, the program has come under increasing attack as being unfair to working wives.[5] Working married women are generally eligible for benefits both as insured workers and as dependent spouses. Entitlement to more than one benefit type is called "dual entitlement." According to the dual-entitlement provision, working spouses are prohibited from receiving two benefits (worker and, for example, wife benefits, widow benefits, or divorced wife benefits) in full. Therefore, the dually entitled spouse receives only the larger of the two benefits. For instance, if the wage earner is married, the spouse may receive a benefit equal to half the wage earner's benefit, unless the spouse would receive a higher benefit on the basis of her (his) individual earnings. The forfeiting of the other benefit has given rise to the notion that the working wife's benefits as an insured worker duplicate her benefits as a dependent.[6] In many cases, the working wives' benefits are about the same as if they never worked outside the home.

Issues of fairness are raised about the treatment of two-earner couples compared with one-earner couples. Many consider it unfair that under the current law, a working husband and a working wife often receive less in retirement than a couple with the same average lifetime earnings credits earned entirely by one spouse. Consider the following 1986 hypothetical example: in family A, the husband retired in 1986 with average indexed monthly earnings (AIME) of $1,600, and his wife did not participate in the labor force (her AIME equals zero).[7] In family B, the couple also has a combined AIME of $1,600; however, the wife's 1986 AIME is $640 and her husband's 1986 AIME is $960. For simplicity, assume all four individuals retire at age 65. The husband's benefit in family A is $684, while his wife is eligible for a spousal benefit equal to 50 percent of her husband's $684, or $342. Family A's combined retirement benefit is $1,026. In family B, the husband's benefit is $479, and his wife is eligible for either a spousal benefit of $240 or a worker benefit of $377 (a marginal gain of $137 over her spousal benefit). Because the wife's worker benefits exceed her dependent wife benefit, family B's combined benefit would be

$856. Family A receives $170 more benefits than family B (a 20-percent benefit advantage).[8]

The marriage duration requirement of 10 years for eligibility for divorced wife benefits also results in a fairness issue. A divorced woman generally derives no Social Security benefits from earnings of a former husband if the marriage lasted less than 10 years.[9] However, if the marriage lasted longer than 10 years, then she may receive a divorced wife benefit on the basis of his entire earnings record. The benefit level is equal to one-half of his insured worker benefit. She is not entitled to divorced wife benefits until the divorced spouse retires. The arbitrariness of the 10-year rule is frequently challenged on both equity and adequacy grounds.

A final fairness issue is the claimed inequity of the earnings or retirement test and the adjustment for postponing retirement. The earnings test limits the amount of earnings a beneficiary may receive from work-related earnings without facing a reduction in retirement benefits. More specifically, if an entitled beneficiary, aged 65 to 72 (70 after 1982), both collects retirement benefits and earns labor income in excess of the normal exempt amount (equalling $7,800 per year in 1986), her benefits will be withheld at a rate of $1 in benefits for every $2 in earnings over the exempt level.[10] In effect, the earnings test discourages beneficiaries from earning income above the legislated level.[11] Opponents of the earnings test argue it is unfair because it penalizes workers who contribute to society's productive capacity and who contribute to the OASI fund after retirement. Workers who work beyond retirement age and abstain from collecting retirement benefits are rewarded by having their benefit level adjusted upward by a monthly delayed retirement credit. Under the 1972 legislation, a worker's benefit could increase by 1 percent per year if she delayed retiring at age 65.[12] Monthly credits stop at age 72 (70 in 1983). At its 1972 level, the delayed retirement credit was insufficient to equalize the present value of the worker's benefit stream. Consequently, the delayed retirement credit and the earnings test tend to discourage working beyond retirement age.

Issues of unequal treatment arise from the redistribution objective. This book does not address the legitimacy of the redistribution objective; instead, it seeks to examine the program's effectiveness in redistributing income within and across retirement cohorts and to examine the magnitude of the inequities within the system. Five interrelated issues are investigated: 1) Does the OAI portion of the Social Security program redistribute income in favor of low-income beneficiaries and earlier retirement cohorts? 2) Does the current OAI program redistribute benefits in favor of women as a group at the expense of their male counterparts?

3) How does the wife's work status affect the distribution of OAI benefits within and across family types? 4) How does marital status affect the distribution of OAI benefits? 5) Are spousal benefits distributed principally to needy, dependent spouses? Answers to these questions are needed to assess the effectiveness of the current OAI program in satisfying its intended objectives and to shed light on inequities and inadequacies resulting from specific provisions in the law.

The distributional impact of the OAI program is isolated by disentangling or decoupling the insurance portion of the OAI benefits from the redistribution portion. The insurance disentanglement employs the actuarial standard of Burkhauser and Warlick (1981), whereby a retired worker's 1972 OASI benefit level is compared to the benefit level the worker would have received from purchasing an actuarially fair life annuity with his or her accumulated OASI contribution on the date of retirement. (Burkhauser and Warlick define this difference as the "transfer component.") The life-cycle framework devised by Burkhauser and Warlick is modified to account for the monthly disbursement of OAI benefits, price indexing, and different mortality expectations. This approach allows us to measure the distributional effects of the progressive benefit formula, spousal benefits, and price indexing.

Chapter 1 presents a brief historical overview of the OAI program and identifies features of the law to be examined in this study. Evidence from previous empirical studies investigating the distributional impact of the Social Security program are discussed in chapter 2. The life-cycle model and conditions for an actuarially fair retirement system are presented in chapter 3. In chapter 4, the assumptions underpinning the model, the data set and sorting technique, computational formulas, annuity-type counterfactuals, and redistribution estimates are briefly explained. Descriptive evidence on intra- and intergenerational redistribution are presented in chapter 5. Generalized quadratic regression models by marital status and a detailed discussion of the model variables are presented in chapter 6. In chapter 7, evidence from the estimation of the regression models is presented and interpreted. Summary, conclusions, and policy recommendations appear in chapter 8.

1

Historical Overview of the Old-Age Insurance Program

The Social Security program in the United States is a dynamic federal income maintenance program that has evolved over its brief 50-year history from a strictly worker-only retirement program to a full-fledged, comprehensive old-age social insurance program.[1] The old-age program developed in 1935 provided retirement benefits to covered workers only. Benefit levels were a function of total covered wages earned by the worker over her work history and were financed by a flat-rate payroll tax levied on the employee and employer. Although the OAI program was partially funded, it was not distributionally neutral. Initial benefit levels were determined by a mildly progressive benefit formula, and benefit payments were not adjusted to reflect different life expectancies of male and female beneficiaries. Hence, even in the early years of the program (prior to 1940, when the first benefits were paid), some redistribution within a cohort, though not across cohorts, was mandated.

The Spousal Benefit Provision

A major drawback to the initial program was its relative ineffectiveness in providing adequate income protection for dependents of covered workers and soon-to-be and already retired workers. Incremental changes in benefit coverage and funding principles were introduced in the form of amendments to the Social Security Act of 1935 to enhance the effectiveness of the program in pursuing the goal of income adequacy for aged persons—the nation's most identifiable impoverished group. The 1939 amendments provided spousal and survivor benefits for women married to covered workers.

The 1937–1939 Advisory Council's recommendation for noncontributory, supplemental security benefits to wives and widows of covered workers was a conscious attempt to ameliorate the economic hardships imposed on this group of women because of the incidental retirement or death of the primary earner who, at that time, did not have a sufficient earnings history to satisfy his own economic needs at retirement, let alone those of his dependents.[2] The receipt and absolute size of the supplemental benefits were linked to the husband's earnings history, preserving the illusion of an insurance program. The supplemental benefits provided family protection, although contributions were based on an individual worker's employment and earnings history exclusively. The OAI program legislated in 1939, and to a large extent operating today, effectively subsidized the traditional family structure characteristic of that time period. It is, however, important to note that the Council's recommendation was reflective of the sociocultural-socioeconomic milieu of the 1930s.

The typical American family in the late 1930s was characterized by a lifelong marriage in which the female assumed the primary responsibility for nurturance and home management and the male assumed the breadwinner role. Married women as a group had weak labor force attachment and, as a consequence, were disproportionately represented outside the labor force. In 1939, only one out of four married women worked outside the home, the three out of 20 households had both husband and wife employed outside the home simultaneously. Most women, therefore, lacked independent OAI protection. The presumption of dependency on behalf of all women was consistent with demographic characteristics and did eliminate a severe inadequacy present in the original version of the strictly worker-only retirement program.

The Council realized that in the near future, and especially in the distant future, married women would be dually entitled to both primary and spousal retirement benefits. The provision of overlapping benefits to married women as independent earners and dependent spouses was inconsistent with the intent of the noncontributory, supplemental security benefit provisions—protecting a needy group from economic hardship resulting from the breadwinner's retirement or death. To avoid the overlapping benefit problem, the dual-entitlement provision was introduced in conjunction with supplemental benefits as a variant of a means test. According to the dual-entitlement provision, if a married woman is entitled to two benefits simultaneously—primary and spousal (survivor)—she will receive the larger of the two benefits. The base of her benefits is her own primary benefit amount, which is then augmented by the difference between her supplemental benefit and primary benefit amounts. The dual-entitlement provision was a noncontroversial addition to the program because it pertained to a small fraction of the entire beneficiary population and was consistent with the generally accepted social adequacy goal of the program.[3]

As mentioned above, the provision of spousal and survivor benefits to women married to covered workers in accordance with the dual-entitlement rule was noncontroversial in light of the demographic characteristics of the 1930s, 1940s, and 1950s. However, as women, especially married women, increased their participation in the labor force, a greater proportion of female beneficiaries qualified for independent as well as dependent benefits.[4] Since the dual-entitlement provision guarantees the dually entitled woman the larger of the two benefits, she must forego the other benefit to which she is entitled. The design of the program gives preferential treatment to dependent, nonworking married women vis-à-vis independent, working married women. A nonworking married woman receives dependent spousal benefits (equal to 50 percent of her husband's primary insurance amount [PIA]) at a zero marginal cost, whereas a working married woman receives either dependent spousal benefits at a marginal cost equal to her total OAI contributions or primary worker benefits at a marginal cost equal to 50 percent of her husband's PIA.

A working married woman may, either totally or fractionally, duplicate protection already afforded to her when classified as a dependent on her husband's account. Hence, the dual-entitlement provision acts as an implicit tax on the working married woman, since she receives only marginal accretions to her benefit level in return for her contributions into the program (i.e., she purchases "redundant" retirement insurance). The dual-entitlement provision implicitly penalizes working women for seeking financial independence and subsidizes the financial dependency of nonworking married women. The effect of the dual-entitlement provision may, especially in light of legislated increases in the payroll tax and the relatively low earnings potential of most females, have an increasingly severe work-disincentive effect and, in addition, may erode the progress women as a group have made in achieving financial independence.

In addition to generating inequities among married women who have made different labor-homemaker decisions, the provision of noncontributory, supplemental benefits generates inequities across household types, depending on marital status and the division of earnings within the household. A two-earner household (a household where the husband and wife are gainfully employed outside the home) with earnings equal to a one-earner household will receive lower combined benefits relative to a one-earner household if the combined earnings of the two-earner unit is less than the taxable maximum for one worker. A two-earner household receives higher benefits compared to a one-earner household when their combined earnings are greater than the taxable maximum for a single earner; however, the two-earner couple pays more in the form of contributions to receive the higher benefit level (Bixby, 1972). The inequities between the one-earner and two-earner households have become more pronounced in light of the historic four-decade upswing in the employment participation of women.

Single persons of either sex are placed in a financially inferior position in a retirement program that provides family protection based on an individual worker financing scheme. Single households are assigned the same tax liability as married households; however, the married household is afforded a greater package of benefits. Single and married workers are treated equally on the contribution side of the program, but they are treated as unequals on the benefit side, since the married household is eligible for dependent benefits not similarly extended to a single person.[5]

The inequities resulting from the 1939 amendments may, at first blush, appear justified in light of the social adequacy objective. However, the features of the program and the incidental inequities must be juxtaposed to modern demographic characteristics to ascertain whether the actual effect of the law is consistent with its intent. Payment of spousal benefits presumes the financial dependency of the married woman and a traditional family structure. The traditional 1939 family does not typify the family of the 1980s or of the future. The modern family is characterized by interdependency rather than dependency. That is, the typical family today is an interdependent economic unit in which partners of either sex have occupational choice and, to a large extent, are not forced to assume stereotypical roles mandated by societal norms. Women as a group are exercising their right to occupational choice and seeking covered employment outside the home.[6] This protracted trend will intensify the inequities among women who have made different labor-homemaker decisions. These inequities are a direct result of noncontributory, supplemental security benefits coupled with the dual-entitlement provision.

There remains a shrinking proportion of women who choose to be homemakers and, therefore, who need income protection in their retirement years.[7] According to the OAI program, the group of modern-day homemakers is presumed to be an identifiably needy group. Information on the pattern of lifetime work for married women is incomplete; however, most empirical evidence suggests that there is an inverse relationship between family income (net of the wife's earnings) and a wife's labor force participation (Boskin, 1973; Cain, 1966; Garfinkel and Masters, 1977). This evidence suggests that the homemaker choice is a more viable option for high income families, which would tend to refute the needy-group argument supporting the provision of noncontributory, supplementary benefits. Holden (1979), using a single-period analysis, found that supplemental benefits were disbursed proportionately to couples in all income categories. Thus, spousal benefits were being distributed to spouses who were not needy according to poverty standards. According to Holden, "supplemental spousal benefits are not paid primarily to beneficiary couples most in need of additional income. Poor couples receive less than their expected share of these benefits based on the percentage of couples who are poor" (Holden, 1982, p. 48).

This book addresses this issue in a life-cycle context to determine if supplemental benefits adequately serve the 1939 objective of protecting a group of aged persons experiencing economic hardship. In addition, sex differentials in survivorship are employed to determine if women as a group are made differentially better off relative to their male counterparts due to the fact that OAI benefits are not adjusted to account for different life expectancies between men and women of the same age.

Progressive Benefit Formula

Traditional insurance funding principles were abandoned in 1939 for deficit financing, or what is more commonly referred to as "pay as you go" financing. The deficit financing provision mandated intergenerational transfers from the currently working population to the retired, nonworking population.[8] The disbursement of benefits to retired persons is based on a progressive benefit formula. The formula has become slightly more progressive over time.

The OAI program, by design, favors low-income households through the retirement benefit formula used to determine the worker's primary insurance amount (PIA) from her average monthly earnings (AME).[9] The retirement benefit formula is structured to pay higher marginal and average benefit rates as the benefit base (AME) decreases. Therefore, the replacement rate (the ratio of retirement benefits to preretirement earnings) is higher for low-income households relative to high-income households. High-income households, however, receive more cash benefits per month in absolute dollars.

The original OAI benefit formula was mildly progressive. The formula applied to average monthly earnings limited to $250 and paid 40 percent of the first $50, plus 10 percent of the next $200. This formula has been periodically revised to favor low-income households. In 1972, the formula paid 108.01 percent of the first $110, plus 39.39 percent of the next $290, plus 36.71 percent of the next $150, plus 43.15 percent of the next $100, plus 24 percent of the next $100, plus 20 percent of the next $250.[10]

This study examines the distributional impact of the progressive benefit formula to ascertain whether, in fact, low-income beneficiaries receive preferential treatment in the disbursement of benefits vis-à-vis high-income beneficiaries. The progressivity of the benefit formula has been disputed because of empirical evidence suggesting that socioeconomic characteristics influence life contingencies.[11]

The Actuarial Reduction for Early Retirement

The permanent actuarial reduction in the monthly benefit amount payable on entitlement applies to retired workers and dependents aged 62 to 64.[12] The intent of this provision was to equalize the total actuarial value of benefits received by the beneficiary independent of the age of retirement.[13] In 1956, provisions were added to the law permitting female beneficiaries to accept retirement benefits at age 62. If the female beneficiary applies for early primary benefits (in advance of age 65), her PIA is reduced by 5/9 of 1 percent per month under age 65 (maximum reduction of 20 percent).[14] Dependents benefits are reduced by 25/36 of 1 percent per month under age 65 (maximum reduction of 25 percent). Identical provisions were extended to male beneficiaries in 1961.

The Delayed Retirement Credit

The benefit level (PIA) is adjusted upward if the primary beneficiary elects to retire after age 65. Like the actuarial reduction provision, the accretion feature was intended to equalize the actuarial value of the benefit stream independent of the age of retirement. Prior to 1983, a covered worker's benefit level was adjusted upward if she remained actively employed and she did not accept retirement between ages 65 and 72. Benefits were increased by 1/12 of 1 percent for every month the covered worker postponed retirement after age 65.[15] Accretions in benefit levels were truncated at age 72. This adjustment in benefits for delaying retirement is less than the actuarial adjustment for the shorter life expectancies of older beneficiaries; hence, the postponement of retirement is translated into a real loss in benefits over the remaining life span.[16] However, under the 1983 legislation, the credit for delayed retirement will increase gradually to 8 percent per year between 1990 and 2008. By 2008, the delayed retirement credit should, on average, equalize the present value of future benefits.[17]

The Earnings Test

The earnings or retirement test is a type of means test that reduces benefits to beneficiaries who continue to work past the age of 65. An earnings test has been in effect since 1935. According to the 1935 earnings test, all retirement benefits would be withheld if the beneficiary received *any* labor earnings during retirement. The extortionate nature of this test was, however, relaxed prior to the payment of the first benefits in 1940. The 1939 version of the earnings test permitted labor-related earnings up to $15 per month without the loss of retirement benefits; however, all benefits were forfeited if earnings exceeded $15. Since 1939, the earnings limit has been increased periodically.

In 1972, retirement benefits were reduced if the beneficiary remained employed after receiving retirement benefits and her earnings exceeded 19 percent of the annual taxable maximum. Benefits were reduced by $1 for every $2 of postretirement earnings between $1,680 and $2,880, but benefits were reduced by $1 for every $1 of earnings above $2,880.[18] However, benefits were not reduced for worker-beneficiaries who were 72 or older in 1972.[19]

From a policy point of view, the earnings test is consistent with the basic purpose of Social Security, which is to fractionally replace lost earnings because the aged worker retires from the labor force. But, from the beginning, the earnings test has been controversial and strongly criticized. The "$1 for $2 and $1 for $1" withholding rate (or "$1 for $2" withholding rate since 1973) has been criticized because the withholding rate applies to labor income only (excluding nonwork income sources like dividends, rents, and pension payments) and because it discourages healthy older persons from seeking gainful employment in the market.

The burden of the 50- to 100-percent withholding rate falls heaviest on the low-income aged because of their greater reliance on Social Security and employment earnings for financial security during retirement. Studies of the financial holdings of the aged show that most low-income persons do not have access to private pensions, private insurance, savings, and other nonwork income sources to augment their retirement benefits (Freidman and Sjogren, 1981; Murray, 1972; Sherman, 1973). Most evidence suggests that the financial status of low-income persons remains unchanged at the outset of retirement in spite of "social security" for several reasons: 1) retirement benefits only partially replace employment earnings, 2) retirement benefits are reduced if the retiree has supplemental postretirement earnings in excess of the earnings ceiling, and 3) low-income persons generally have insufficient nonwork income sources.

The Cost-of-Living Adjustment

In the mid-1960s, influential persons in Congress and the executive branch began to push for a bigger role for Social Security as an income source for the elderly. Congress approved benefit increases of 15 percent in 1969, 10 percent in 1971, and 20 percent in July 1972. In October 1972, Congress passed the Social Security Amendments of 1972. The major features of this legislation were provisions for indexing the wage base used in computing initial benefits and for using the consumer price index (CPI) to adjust payments to current beneficiaries. Although automatic indexing was legislated in 1972, it did not become effective until 1975. Legislated increases were substituted for automatic indexing in 1973 and 1974.[20] Benefits paid to current beneficiaries are annually indexed whenever the CPI rises by more than 3 percent.[21]

The Social Security system is intended to insure beneficiaries against the economic risk of longevity. Indexing of benefits enhances this form of insurance in an inflationary environment. Because women as a group have a longer life expectancy than men, they receive on average more benefits from indexing. Indexing of benefits for retired workers keeps intact the relative benefit structure, since all benefit streams are adjusted by the same index.

2

Intrageneration and Intergeneration Redistribution: The Empirical Evidence

Although the objective characteristics of the OAI program, including the extent of insurance protection, have changed over time, its initial intent of providing adequate protection against long-term uncertainties associated with the cessation of labor force participation because of old age has remained undiminished. Specific features added to the program over time, compromising its 1935 insurance principles, ultimately influence the estimated size of the redistribution component. However, the gradual shifting toward social adequacy goals has engendered inequities in the program's operation. The alleged inequities include the preferential treatment of women, traditional family structures, low-income households, and nonworking persons aged 62 to 72 (70 after 1982). A more subtle, but no less important, inequity incidental to the program concerns differential survivorship. Mortality studies indicate that specific socioeconomic characteristics influence survivor probabilities (Antonovsky, 1972; Gove, 1973; Kitagawa and Hauser, 1973; Metropolitan Life, 1975).[1] In a retirement program that pays benefits for the duration of life, persons with lower survivor probabilities (or shorter life expectancies), as reflected by specific, identifiable socioeconomic factors, subsidize persons with relatively higher survivor probabilities (or longer life expectancies).[2]

The effects of these inequities (program- and worker-specific) have been investigated in numerous empirical studies using different conceptual frameworks, data bases (representative individual and individual case history approaches), model assumptions, and equity measures. However, independent of the methodology employed, virtually all empirical studies indicate that Social Security beneficiaries retiring prior to 1975 received above-normal rates of return on their contribution dollars, independent of income classification and other socioeconomic characteristics. Although there is consensus on the "money's worth" issue prior to 1975, there is less agreement concerning the overall progressivity of the program and concerning the expected return on contributions for future retirees.

The distributional impact of the Social Security program has intrigued and challenged researchers for many years. In this chapter, the major empirical studies on intra- and intergenerational redistribution from 1970 to present are examined. The discussion begins with a description of three conceptual frameworks used to evaluate the program's performance. Then, the results of several representative studies on the distributional impact of the Social Security system are examined using the conceptual framework typology. The chapter closes with a summary discussion of the empirical evidence.

Conceptual Frameworks

Thompson (1983) describes three competing conceptual frameworks for analyzing the Social Security system: the tax-transfer model, the insurance model, and the annuity-welfare model.[3] The least prominent framework, which Thompson calls the tax-transfer model of Social Security, decomposes the program into two separate and unrelated government programs—benefit transfers (expenditures) and payroll tax contributions (revenues). Each program is evaluated separately using either standard principles of taxation (e.g., ability to pay) or welfare criteria (e.g., demonstrated need). According to the tax-transfer model, there is no reason to expect benefits received by a retired beneficiary to bear any direct or indirect relationship to taxes paid by the beneficiary. Only a few recently published studies conform to the tax-transfer framework (Danziger, 1977; Danziger and Plotnick, 1975; Lampman, 1971; Ozawa, 1976).

Most published studies reflect the insurance model. The insurance model of the Social Security system compares the tax price of the benefit package to the expected value of the insurance protection (e.g., the present discounted value of the retirement benefit stream). According to this conceptualization, the Social Security program is envisaged as the pooling among covered workers of the risk of earnings loss because of an uncertain event—retirement, disability, or death. The relationship between benefits and contributions is measured using lifetime benefit-contribution ratios, present value of net benefits (net Social Security wealth), or internal rates of return. The insurance framework is reflected in studies by Aaron (1977); Brittain (1972a); Campbell and Campbell (1967); Chen and Chu (1974); Ferrara and Lott (1985); Freiden, Leimer, and Hoffman (1976); Hurd and Shoven (1983); Leimer and Petri (1981); Moffit (1982); Okonkwo (1976); Ozawa (1982); and Pellechio and Goodfellow (1983).

The third conceptual framework is the annuity-welfare model of Social Security, which decouples the strictly insurance portion of the retirement benefit (i.e., the benefit portion the beneficiary actually paid for) from the redistribution or transfer portion. Like the insurance model, the annuity-welfare model relies on a life-cycle framework of the retirement system. However, unlike the insurance model, the annuity-welfare model uses an actuarial standard of fairness to determine how much a retired worker would receive from an actuarially fair retirement system. The transfer component is then isolated by comparing the actual benefits paid to a beneficiary (or retirement cohort) with what she would receive from an annuity purchased at retirement with compounded OAI tax contributions. Each portion of the benefit is then analyzed separately. This conceptualization of the Social Security program has become more prominent in empirical studies on the distributional impact of the program since the early 1980s (Burkhauser and Warlick, 1981).

Previous Empirical Evidence

The Tax-Transfer Model

Analysts using the tax-transfer model found the Social Security program to be the most effective U.S. government program in redistributing income to an impoverished group (Danziger, 1977; Danziger and Plotnick, 1975; Lampman, 1971; Ozawa, 1976). The success of the Social Security program in decreasing income inequality can be explained by several factors. First, the progressive benefit formula replaces a larger percentage of the low-wage earner's preretirement earnings than for the high-wage earner. The redistributive function of the formula would tend to reduce postretirement income differentials within a retirement cohort, ceteris paribus. Second, a large percentage of the aged is eligible for retirement benefits. The blanket coverage of the program enhances the income position of all income classes within a retirement cohort and improves their income standing relative to the working population.

A third factor pertains to the absolute size of the transfers to the aged. Public assistance is considered to be the most economically efficient program of all income maintenance programs; however, Social Security, while being economically less efficient, has the greatest redistributive impact. This apparent disparity between economic efficiency and redistributive impact is best explained by the following analogy: a 100-percent share of a peanut is still a peanut, but a 50-percent share of an elephant is half an elephant (Ozawa, 1976). That is, the amount of total benefits received by the targeted population depends on economic efficiency and the total amount of the outlay. In 1983, the Social Security (OASDI) program paid out $168 billion in cash benefits compared to cash benefits totaling $86 billion under public aid (public assistance, SSI, food stamps, work relief, etc.).

The last factor to be discussed concerns the use of single-period methodology to assess the performance of a life-cycle program. Single-period investigations into the performance of the Social Security program assess the redistributive impact of the program by examining the degree of income inequality before and after the payment of retirement benefits. Clearly, this approach fails to account for the income-smoothing function of the program; hence, it tends to overstate the redistributive impact of the program.[4] Redistribution conclusions from single-period analyses are strongly disputed by researchers using life-cycle models of the OAI program.

The Insurance Model

Many researchers have investigated the effect of the Social Security program (OAI, OASI, and OASDI) on the distribution of lifetime income within a life-cycle framework using the insurance model of the program. The distributional impact has been measured in terms of lifetime internal rates of return, lifetime contribution-benefit ratios, and net Social Security wealth. The absolute size of the distributional impact measure has been found to be sensitive to specific identifiable factors, such as date of retirement, marital status, sex, race, income class, education level, and age at entry and retirement. The empirical estimates of redistribution also depend on the richness of the data base and on the model assumptions regarding benefit inclusion, payroll tax shifting, projected earnings trajectories, life expectancy tables, and market interest rates. Several of the major findings from studies using each measure are discussed below.

Internal rates of return. The standard method for calculating an individual's expected *future* return from the Social Security program is to construct benefit and contribution streams for hypothetical or representative workers. An internal rate of return statistic is calculated by finding the interest rate that equalizes the compounded value of total contributions paid over the work history and the present value of expected stream of retirement benefits received after retirement.

Studies investigating the extent to which the Social Security program redistributes lifetime income among subgroups of an age cohort using an internal rate of return measure have generally found the internal rate of return on OAI (OASI, OASDI) contributions to be negatively related to income, date of retirement, age at retirement (relative to age 65), and education level, and positively related to age at entry. Internal rates of return also have been found to be higher for women, nonwhite races, and married persons. Furthermore, rates of return were found to be higher for all subgroups the smaller the assumed backward shifting of the employer's share of the payroll tax. Similarly, the absolute size of the rate of return for specific socioeconomic groups varied depending on the extent to which life expectancy tables were disaggregated. Also, real internal rates of return were found to be significantly smaller than nominal rates; the gap between the real and nominal measures increased when the inflation rate was higher than the annual rate of growth of retirement benefits.

The most comprehensive studies using the internal rate of return measure have been conducted by Okonkwo (1976), Freiden, Leimer, and Hoffman (1976), Leimer and Petri (1981), Hurd and Shoven (1983), and Ferrara and Lott (1985). With the exception of Freiden, Leimer, and Hoffman, all these studies calculated expected rates of return for hypothetical workers. The projected rates may be compared within and across retirement cohorts to assess how current and future retirees fare under the program, and they may be compared with alternative yields on alternative private market savings instruments.

Okonkwo (1976) calculated internal rates for 1974 retirees using longitudinal age-earnings profiles derived from a combined time series and cross sections of decennial U.S. population census data (1939–1969) on income and life expectancies disaggregated by sex, race, and education levels. He found higher rates of return for couples relative to single persons, nonwhites relative to whites, and households located in the South relative to those in the North. He also found that rates of return varied inversely with education level. For example, workers with eight years of schooling received the highest return on their tax contributions, and workers with 16 or more years of schooling received the lowest return, independent of race, marital status, region, sex, or type of tax (OAI, OASDI). Expected real rates of return for hypothetical workers retiring in 1974 ranged from 11.2 percent (one-earner couples with eight years of education located in the South) to 6.7 percent (single male with 16 or more years of education located in the South). Okonkwo concludes that the Social Security program was progressive for 1974 retirees. He found that the program redistributed income to low-income nonwhites and whites as intended by the law, but the redistribution effect was dampened by differential survivorship probabilities. That is, the degree of redistribution, measured by the gap between the rates of return across education levels, for the white subgroup was reduced by the longer life expectancies for white persons with more education. No positive relationship between educational attainment and longevity was observed for nonwhites.

Freiden, Leimer, and Hoffman (1976) used earnings and benefit data from the Continuous Work History Survey and survivorship probabilities disaggregated by age, sex, and race to calculate internal rates of return. Earnings and benefit streams were constructed for a sample of case histories of workers who retired from 1967 to 1970. Longitudinal earnings profiles and retirement ages were known for each worker. Internal rates of return were calculated for worker-only beneficiaries and then aggregated over key individual characteristics (sex, race, income, and retirement year). The authors found the OAI portion of the program to be strongly progressive for recent retirees. Significantly higher rates of return were found for low-income subgroups relative to high-income subgroups and for women relative to men. Average rates of return for workers retiring at age 65 ranged from 29 percent for low-earning women to 8.5 percent for high-earning men.

Leimer and Petri (1981) examined intergenerational effects of Social Security policy in a long-term context using internal rates of return. Projected internal rates of return for each cohort born between 1917 and 2000 were calculated from a new long-run microsimulation model of the Social Security system and the economy. The authors projected that the high real rates of return for individuals born in 1917 (approximately 7 percent) would decline monotonically over time. They also projected real rates of return on payroll tax contributions between 2 and 3 percent for cohorts retiring after 2005 (workers born after 1940). Their findings are based on assumptions adopted for the 1980 Social Security long-range cost projections and age-detailed earnings, tax, and benefit projections.

Hurd and Shoven (1983) estimated rates of return for six synthetic age cohorts, four household types, and three levels of earnings records. Their study examined intra- and intergenerational transfers of retirement cohorts who reach age 65 in 10-year intervals from 1970 through 2020. The household types considered consisted of single males, single females, one-earner couples, and two-earner couples. Earnings profiles of low, median, and high were derived from projected earnings trajectories based on 1937–1977 median annual earnings of men and women. Their results are consistent with earlier studies. Within all retirement cohorts, real rates of return were found to consistently decline as earnings increased for all representative cases. For 1970, the difference between low and high earners ranged from 2.1 percentage points for single males, one-earner, and two-earner couples to 4.0 percentage points for single women. These patterns in computed real rates of return suggest that the Social Security program is progressive over individual life cycles for past and future retirees. The authors also found that future rates of return decline steadily from 1970 to 2020.

The study by Ferrara and Lott (1985) calculated future rates of return for workers entering the work force in 1983. To allow for intragenerational comparisons, the representative families were assumed to differ by earnings level (minimum wage, average earnings, and maximum taxable earnings), employment age (18, 22, and 24), and marital status (single, married-two-earner, and married-one-earner). Workers were assumed to retire at age 67. The 1983 Social Security Trustee Report intermediate IIB projections were used to project future payroll tax and benefit streams. The authors calculated real rates of return ranging from −1.5 to 2.75 percent on tax contributions. Rates of return were highest for low-income, one-earner couples, estimated at 2.75 percent. Yields were negative for high-earner single workers and for other family units with high earnings.

Lifetime contribution-benefit ratios. Examination of the relationship between Social Security contributions and benefits using a contribution (tax)-benefit (C-B) ratio measure were undertaken by Brittain (1972a), Chen and Chu (1974), and Aaron (1977). These studies deal with C-B analyses for persons who already retired and/or persons who expect to retire in the distant future. All three studies are based on simulations for hypothetical workers. The C-B study results are generally consistent with the internal rate of return study results. The one exception pertains to the Aaron finding of a positive relationship between the benefit-contribution (B-C) ratio and income. Aaron's results cast doubt on the future progressivity of the program.

Contribution-benefit ratios are computed by dividing the compounded value of contributions paid over the worker's life cycle by the present value of expected benefits received after retirement. An individual with a C-B ratio less than unity is a Social Security gainer; the smaller the ratio, the larger the gain. A C-B ratio greater than unity indicates the individual is a Social Security loser. The larger the ratio, the greater the loss. The gainer-loser relationship is reversed when a benefit-contribution (B-C) ratio is estimated.

Brittain (1972a) calculated projected C-B ratios using a simple growth model that approximated the 1966 Social Security system. The model assumed fixed real rates of growth of average earnings and benefits. The benefit stream was adjusted to reflect differential mortality rates of men and women. All workers paid the average annual tax, but workers entered the labor force at different ages. Workers entered the labor force in 1966 at age 18 or 22. Both worker types retired at age 65. Given the economic and demographic assumptions, Brittain computed average lifetime C-B ratios for beneficiaries of average earnings ranging from 0.36 to 2.08. High earnings growth rates, low interest rates, low-cost projections, and later starting age resulted in lower C-B ratios. Lower ratios were also estimated for married couples relative to single individuals and for women relative to men.[5]

Chen and Chu (1974) used a microsimulation model to compute OASI C-B ratios for 1974 retirees and 1974 entrants (aged 18 and 22). Hypothetical workers were assumed to earn either average annual earnings or annual earnings equal to the maximum taxable earnings. Benefit streams were constructed using 1974 program provisions and Social Security Administration graduated mortality rates disaggregated by age, sex, and race. Their simulated results indicated that the 1974 retirees gained on their Social Security taxes. All 1974 retiree C-B ratios were well below one, ranging from 0.08 to 0.46. Ratios were lower for average earners relative to maximum earners, couples relative to single workers (worker benefit only), 1974 retirees relative to 1974 entrants, and 1974 entrants aged 22 relative to 1974 entrants aged 18. For the 1974 entrants, the computed C-B ratios showed them to be gainers, but the magnitude of the gain was considerably smaller than that of the 1974 retirees.[6]

The study by Aaron (1977) relied on projected longitudinal earnings for representative workers entering the labor force after 1966. His longitudinal age-earnings profiles were derived by extrapolating a 1966 cross sectional earnings profile reported in the 1967 *Survey of Economic Opportunity.* Survivorship probabilities were disaggregated by race, sex, marital status, education, and income. Benefit levels were based on the 1967 benefit formula. The representative worker retired at age 65 in the year 2017. In sharp contrast with all previously mentioned studies, Aaron found the old-age insurance portion of the Social Secuirty program to be regressive for future retirees. Aaron's results show that the relative B-C ratios rise with education for a cohort of white households aged 18 in 1970. The reversing pattern held across all white households—for one- and two-earner couples and for male and female single workers. Nonwhite households were found to have irregularly progressive patterns. Aaron concludes that the enhanced life expectancy associated with more years of schooling fully or partially offsets the progressivity built into the retirement benefit formula, compromising the redistributional intent of the program.

Net Social Security wealth. Net Social Security wealth (NSSW) is defined as the difference between the present value of retirement benefits and tax contributions. The value of NSSW is zero in an actuarially fair system. If the calculated value is positive, then the worker (or cohort) has gained financially from participating in the program over the life cycle. On the other hand, a negative NSSW value indicates the worker (or cohort) is a net loser. Inter- and intragenerational transfers can be inferred from this residual measure of value.

Recent studies by Moffit (1982) and Pellechio and Goodfellow (1983) generated NSSW values for hypothetical workers from microsimulation models. Moffit's is the only insurance model study demonstrating that intergenerational transfers have steadily increased for later cohorts. He calculated NSSW for eight cohorts of hypothetical workers entering the labor force between 1942 and 1977. Workers were assumed to differ by date of entry only; hence, only intergenerational comparisons were permitted. NSSW was estimated at time of entry and was expressed in 1967 dollars. Moffit found that 1) all successive cohorts received positive NSSW, 2) the absolute value of wealth *increased* for all retirement cohorts reaching retirement age up to 1977, and 3) the growth rate of NSSW has fallen over time. This is the only simulation study showing an increase in intergenerational transfers for later retirement cohorts.

Pellechio and Goodfellow (1983) developed a simulation model incorporating survival and disability rates, past and projected earnings trajectories, and program parameters to calculate the value of NSSW for hypothetical workers in 1983. They calculated 30 earnings/family-type cells of NSSW for each age cohort of hypothetical workers. Workers were assumed to differ by family status, sex, and earnings level. Three age cohorts were used: age 25, 40, and 55 in 1983. Within each age cohort, five family situations were assumed: single males, single females, one-earner couples where only the wife works, one-earner couples where only the husband works, and two-earner couples. Hypothetical workers were assumed to earn one of six different earnings levels, ranging from $10,000 to $35,700. In keeping with previously mentioned studies (except Moffit's), NSSW was found to decline with age. Also, the number of negative NSSW estimates was found to increase for younger age cohorts (e.g., five negative cells for persons aged 55 in 1983, 15 negative cells for persons aged 40 in 1983, and 17 negative cells for persons aged 25 in 1983). The absolute size of the NSSW measure was highest for one-earner couples where the wife works and lowest for single males.

The Annuity-Welfare Model

The distributional impact of the Social Security program is isolated by decoupling the insurance portion of the beneficiary's retirement benefit from the redistribution (transfer) portion. The decoupling is accomplished by estimating a series of annuity-type counterfactuals—person-specific estimates of actuarially fair payments. The annuity is purchased at retirement with the worker's accumulated payroll tax contributions. The transfer payment is isolated by comparing the beneficiary's actual retirement benefit to the annuity payment. The transfer component equals zero in an actuarially fair system. The attractive feature of this approach is that it focuses on individual equity as viewed over the life cycle of an individual. This approach was first estimated using a sample of beneficiary data by Burkhauser and Warlick (1981). The transfer component measure is also used in the later chapters of this book.

Transfer component. Burkhauser and Warlick drew on a sample of beneficiaries from the 1973 Exact Match File to estimate annuity-type transfer components. Longitudinal earnings data from individual records allowed them to estimate the accumulated value of each worker's OASI payroll tax contributions at time of retirement. They then calculated the annual (nominal) annuity payment that the worker could purchase at retirement with this amount. The size of the annuity payment depends on the accumulated value of OASI taxes and the life expectancy of the worker and dependent spouse, if present. Inter- and intragenerational transfers were measured by subtracting the estimated annuity payment from the retired worker's actual 1972 OASI benefit level. The results were displayed in tabular form by 1972 household income class. Overall, the authors found that all income classes of 1972 beneficiaries received retirement benefits in excess of their annuity payments. The middle-income group of retirees received the largest transfer from the program. They also found that the amount of redistribution, measured in absolute dollars, was roughly equal for high- and low-income beneficiaries. Relative transfers, the transfer component expressed as a percentage of OASI benefits, generally diminished as income increased, although the pattern was reversed for high-income beneficiaries. Burkhauser and Warlick also found that relative transfers were highest for earlier cohorts, confirming the intergenerational results of previously mentioned studies (except Moffit's).

In this study, I have used a modified version of the Burkhauser-Warlick method of measuring redistribution. I have adjusted the life-cycle framework developed by Burkhauser and Warlick to account for the monthly disbursement of OAI benefits, price indexing, and different mortality expectations. Also, I have confined my study to OAI benefits, OAI payroll tax contributions, and the 1962–1972 retirement cohorts. Details of the revised and extended methodology are further described in chapters 3 and 4.

Interpreting the Evidence

The higher rates of return associated with marital status, date of retirement, age at retirement, and income can be explained by the program's design in conjunction with differential survivorship probabilities. Other factors influencing the size of OAI returns, such as sex, race, and education, can be explained by differential survivorship probabilities.

The higher returns associated with marital status are attributable to two independent factors: 1) the OAI program, by design, subsidizes the traditional (one-earner) family structure through the provision of spousal benefits in accordance with the dual-entitlement rule; and 2) married persons, independent of race and sex, have longer life expectancies, on average, than their nonmarried, divorced, or widowed counterparts.

The first factor is related to the program's design, whereby a nonworking married person receives dependent spousal benefits (equal to 50 percent of the spouse's primary insurance amount [PIA])[7] at a zero cost. A working married person, on the other hand, receives dependent spousal benefits at a cost equal to her total payroll tax contributions or primary worker benefits at a cost equal to 50 percent of her spouse's PIA. Recall that according to the dual-entitlement provision, a person entitled to two benefits simultaneously will receive the larger of the two benefits, but she must forego the other benefits to which she is entitled. A similar partiality toward married couples is exposed when single persons are compared to married persons claiming dependents benefits with the same prior contributions. The single person receives a lower rate of return on her (his) initial OAI contributions relative to a married person collecting dependents benefits with the same contributions, since a married person is eligible for dependents benefits not similarly extended to a single person without dependents. Burkhauser (1979), using data from the 1973 Exact Match File, found that one-earner married coules fare better than either two-earner married couples or single individuals, because one-earner couples receive spousal benefits at no additional charge and because single persons are forced to participate in a retirement system designed for married persons.

The second factor pertains to the longer life expectancy of married persons. Mortality studies conclusively show that married persons of each race and sex have longer life expectancies than their nonmarried, divorced, or widowed counterparts (Gove, 1973; Kitagawa and Hauser, 1973; Metropolitan Life, 1975). It is interesting to note that the differences between married and unmarried statuses are much greater for men than for women. For instance, single white males aged 65 and over experienced mortality levels 44 percent greater than those of married white males comparably aged. Similarly, single white females aged 65 and over have mortality levels 9 percent higher than those of comparably aged married white females. A single person has a shorter life expectancy, on average, relative to a married person of roughly the same age, everything else equal. Both of these factors taken together exert upward pressure on the rate of return on payroll tax contributions for the traditional family structure relative to the nontraditional family structure, although married persons (one-earner or two-earner couples) fare better than single persons.

The retirement date factor reflects the relative maturity or immaturity of the retirement program.[8] The first generation of Social Security retirees received exorbitant rates of return on their prior contributions owing to the fact that they had few years of coverage in the program and a relatively long period of benefit collection. Subsequent generations have benefited from the relative immaturity of the program, which made possible extremely low tax rates and frequent increases in benefit levels. As the system matures, meaning the contribution period eclipses the entire work history, the size of the intergenerational transfer and subsequent rates of return on prior contributions will diminish.

Parsons and Munro (1977) show that within the next 50 years the intergenerational transfer will disappear completely; hence, each retirement cohort will distribute among its members the amount of money they initially paid into the program. Freiden, Leimer, and Hoffman (1976) studied the retirement cohorts from 1967 through 1970 focusing on worker-only beneficiaries. Although all coefficients were small, they found that the 1968 retirees' rates of return were 2.27 percent higher than those of the 1967 retirees, whereas the 1969 retirees' rates of return were 1.76 percent lower than those of the 1967 retirees. There was no significant difference found between the rates of return for the 1970 and 1967 retirees. Burkhauser and Warlick (1981) found a general decline in the percentage of redistribution over time. By dividing the 1972 cohort into three age cohorts, 66–67, 72–75, 81–85, they found that the oldest age cohort received the largest intergenerational transfers and that the youngest age cohort received the smallest. The Moffit (1982) study is the only study suggesting that later retirement cohorts have actually received larger transfers from the program.

Income is an important factor in determining the overall progressivity of the OAI program. The program, by design, favors low-income households through the retirement benefit formula used to determine the worker's PIA from her (his) average monthly earnings (AME).[9] The retirement benefit formula is structured to pay higher marginal and average benefit rates as the benefit base (AME) decreases. Therefore, the replacement rate (the ratio of retirement benefits to preretirement earnings) is higher for low-income units relative to high-income units, although high-income units receive more cash benefits per month in absolute dollars. Most studies have found the OAI program to be progressive. Freiden, Leimer, and Hoffman (1976) estimated the elasticity of the internal rate of return with respect to lifetime income for OAI benefits to be −0.278. Other studies using a broader definition of benefits and more disaggregated mortality rates have shown less progressivity than the Freiden study (Okonkwo, 1976; Aaron, 1977). Aaron (1977) concludes the program will be regressive for future retirees.

The retirement age factor influences the size of the return because of the early-retirement and delayed-retirement features of the program. Persons who choose to remain employed between the ages of 65 and 72 receive additional retirement benefits according to the number of incremental months employed during this age period. The PIA is increased by 1/12 of 1 percent for each month retirement is delayed after age 65, with a maximum adjustment of 7 percent if the worker should remain employed until age 72. The accretion to the PIA, however, understates the shorter life expectancy of the worker who delays retirement. Alternatively, the actuarial reduction in the PIA for early retirement (retirement age of 62 to 64) is excessive. Freiden, Leimer, and Hoffman (1976) found that optimum age at retirement, in terms of maximizing the internal rate of return, was 65.

The last factor to influence the rate of return or extent of redistribution is differential mortality rates. The Kitagawa and Hauser study (1973) on differential mortality rates in the United States indicated that socioeconomic factors, especially sex, race, occupation, income, education, and marital status, influence the individual's probability of dying at (surviving to) a specific life age. The effect of marital status on survival was mentioned earlier and, hence, will not be discussed further. Mortality rates were, however, found to be negatively related to income and education, eliciting the opposite effect of the progressive benefit formula on rates of return on payroll tax contributions. Mortality rates were also found to be higher for men relative to women and for nonwhites relative to whites. Other things equal, women, on average, can expect to receive a higher return on their contributions vis-à-vis male counterparts given that women have, on average, longer life expectancies than men. Freiden, Leimer, and Hoffman (1976) found that women can expect rates of return on their OAI contributions that are approximately 8.8 percent higher than men and that nonwhites can expect rates of return approximately 1.9 percent lower than whites, everything else equal.

3

A Formal Specification of the Life-Cycle Model

The life-cycle model used to measure intra- and intergenerational redistribution is described in this chapter. To evaluate the redistribution of the OAI program, the program was divided into two flows of money—an inflow of contributions and an outflow of benefits. During the worker's earning years, she pays in a flow of contributions, in the form of a flat-rate payroll tax, earmarked for the OAI program in exchange for a promise of a steady stream of real (nominal) income in the later phase of her life cycle. The accumulated value of the worker's contribution, TC_i, paid in over the work history is determined using a traditional compounding scheme.[1] The traditional compounding scheme calculates the total OAI contributions, TC_i, credited to the covered worker's account on the date of retirement by

$$TC_i = \sum_{y=B}^{RE} T_{yi} \prod_{j=y}^{RE} (1 + r_j) \tag{3.1}$$

where T_{yi} = OAI contributions in year y for individual i; r_j = annual yield on U.S. government bonds in year j; RE = year of retirement; and B = first year in covered employment.

The value of OAI contributions, T_{yi}, in equation 3.1 depends on the year the income is earned, y, the amount of income earned, E_{yi}, relative to the maximum taxable earnings base, M_y, and the relevant OAI tax rate, t_y. The individual's OAI contributions for the years 1937 through 1950 were determined by (a) $T_{yi} = t_y E_{yi}$ when $E_{yi} \leqslant M_y$; and (b) $T_{yi} = t_y E_{yi} + 1/2 t_y (E_{yi} - M_i)$ when $E_{yi} > M_y$. For the years 1951 through 1954, OAI contributions were determined in three different ways, depending on the type of income earned and the relationship between income earned and the maximum taxable earnings base. In the first case, total earnings are equal to the sum of wages, W_{yi}, plus self-employment income, I_{yi}, but are less than the maximum taxable earnings base ($E_{yi} = W_{yi} + I_{yi} < M_y$).

In this case, OAI contributions are determined by (c) $T_{yi} = t_y W_{yi} + t_{ys} I_{yi}$, where t_{ys} = the self-employment OAI tax rate. The second case pertains to the condition where total earnings exceed the maximum taxable earnings base, but total wages do not ($E_{yi} > M_y$, but $W_{yi} < M_y$); then, (d) $T_{yi} = t_y W_{yi} + t_{ys} (M_y - W_{yi})$. The final case is identical to the pre-1951 formula when wage earnings, W_{yi}, are equal to, less than, or greater than the maximum taxable earnings base. For the years after 1955, total wages are defined as the sum of agricultural and nonagricultural wages. OAI contributions, T_{yi}, are calculated using the 1951–1954 formulas.

The revenue stream marked "contributions" qualifies the worker for primary and spousal benefits provided she satisfies the eligibility criteria established by the Social Security laws effective in the year of retirement. The discounted present value of the expected OAI benefit stream for a single person on the date of retirement is

$$B_i^s = \sum_{K=0}^{99-R} \sum_{t=1}^{12} \frac{{}_{R(12)+K(12)+t}P_{R(12)}\, b_o (1+C)^K}{(1+i)^{K(12)+t}} \tag{3.2}$$

and the discounted present value of a couple's OAI benefit stream is[2]

$$B_i^c = \sum_{K=0}^{99-R} \sum_{t=1}^{12} \frac{Z\, b_o (1+C)^K}{(1+i)^{K(12)+t}} \tag{3.3}$$

where

$$Z = {}_{R(12)+K(12)+t}P^M_{R(12)} + {}_{R(12)+K(12)+t}P^F_{R(12)} - 0.5\{{}_{R(12)+K(12)+t}P^M_{R(12)} \times {}_{R(12)+K(12)+t}P^F_{R(12)}\};$$

t = number of benefit payment periods per year; $99-R$ = number of years in the retirement period; R = the retirement age of the worker and spouse; ${}_{R(12)+K(12)+t}P^M_{R(12)}$ = the probability of the male retiree surviving to life age R(12) + K(12) + t, given he is already life age R(12) (expressed in months); ${}_{R(12)+K(12)+t}P^F_{R(12)}$ = the probability of the female retiree surviving to life age R(12) + K(12) + t, given she is already life age R(12) (expressed in months); b_o = the initial OAI benefit level received at the end of the first month of retirement; C = the expected growth in prices in subsequent years; and i = the discount rate.

The life-cycle model of contributions and benefits represented by equations 3.1 through 3.3 captures the salient features of the OAI program. That is, workers pay in a stream of income during their earning years and receive a stream of income in their retirement years, where the right to the benefit stream depends on their past participation on the contribution side of the existing program. This is not to imply, however, that the contribution and benefit streams have any tangible relationship except that prior contributions qualify the worker for future benefits. The two money streams are not worker-specific and need not be comparable in value. The value of the contribution stream depends on the number of earning years, the placement of the earning years in the work history, the worker's taxable earnings in those years, the OAI contribution rate and base, and the interest rate. The value of the benefit stream depends on the discount rate, the growth in future prices, the retiree's life expectancy, and the initial benefit payment. The value of the initial benefit payment, in turn, depends on the worker's average monthly earnings, the progressive benefit formula, age at retirement, familial characteristics, and post-retirement earnings level.

Redistribution, within the intertemporal framework, is determined by the relationship between the total value of the accumulated contributions (3.1) and the present discounted value of the expected OAI benefit stream (3.2, 3.3). If the condition,

$$TC_i \lessgtr B_i^{s,c}, \tag{3.4}$$

holds for an individual, then the individual is expected, on average, to receive retirement benefits that are greater than (less than) the accumulated value of her OAI contributions. In this case, the OAI program affects the lifetime income stream for the individual (couple) within the retirement cohort. Similarly, redistribution across cohorts occurs if

$$\sum_{i=1}^{n} TC_i \lessgtr \sum_{i=1}^{n} B_i^{s,c}. \tag{3.5}$$

An actuarially fair retirement would satisfy the following two conditions:

$$TC_i = B_i^{s,c} \tag{3.6}$$

and

$$\sum_{i=1}^{n} TC_i = \sum_{i=1}^{n} B_i^{s,c}. \tag{3.7}$$

For instance, if each individual purchases an actuarially fair life annuity with her accumulated contributions, then she can expect, on average, to receive a benefit stream exactly equal to her original lump sum premium (equation 3.6). An annuity purchased with her total OAI contributions at the point of retirement insures the individual against economic risk over an uncertain life span by transferring income from her relatively high-earning years to her low-earning years. The value of the monthly annuity payment depends on the value of the lump sum premium, the annuitant's age at retirement, the discount rate, the survivorship table, and the inflation rate (see chapter 4 for the annuity formulas).

Given the above model and definitions of an actuarially fair retirement program, the beneficiary's benefit level can be divided along functional lines. The actuarial component of the individual's OAI benefit payment is the annuity payment that satisfies equation 3.6. The difference between the retiree's 1972 benefit level (b_o) and the annuity benefit (b_a) would determine the amount of redistribution from the program. The redistribution component for individual i is, therefore, defined as

$$RC_i = b_{oi} - b_{ai}. \tag{3.8}$$

Intergenerational redistribution for cohort I is defined as

$$RC_I = \sum_{i=1}^{n} b_{oi} - \sum_{i=1}^{n} b_{ai}. \tag{3.9}$$

If, for instance, each retirement cohort receives retirement benefits equal to the present value of its OAI tax contributions (equation 3.7), then RC_I will equal zero.

4

Methodological Assumptions Underlying the Estimation of Redistribution

A life-cycle model of the OAI program is employed to preserve the link between prior OAI contributions paid into the program over the worker's earnings history and OAI benefits received by the beneficiary during retirement. The contributory system modeling of Social Security is consistent with the individual equity analysis undertaken in this study. However, it is not meant to imply that the contribution and benefit streams have any tangible relationship except that prior contributions "qualify" the worker for future benefits.

The model discussed in chapter 3 was estimated to examine the impact of differential mortality rates, age at retirement, sex, marital status, income, postretirement earnings, and price indexing on the OAI redistribution component. In this chapter, the assumptions of the model, the data set and sorting technique, computational formulas, annuity-type counterfactuals, and redistribution estimates are briefly discussed.

Fairness Standard

The OAI program can be, and frequently is, evaluated on the basis of two conflicting standards of fairness. If fairness, for instance, is defined as giving more to those persons with a greater relative need, then the social adequacy goal of the program is the main focal point of analysis. The relative need standard of fairness evaluates the program's performance in terms of whether or not greater income protection is extended to those aged persons with greater relative needs, independent of previous OAI contributions. However, if fairness means actuarially fair or, in other words, giving more to those persons with a larger initial investment, then the individual equity goal of the program is emphasized. The relative investment standard of fairness evaluates the performance of the program in terms of actuarially fair rates of return on total OAI contributions. This latter definition of fairness is most frequently used to answer whether an individual beneficiary is receiving his money's worth from the government program.

In this study, an actuarial standard of fairness is employed to determine the benefit amount the covered worker would receive from an actuarially fair retirement program. Benefits in excess of the actuarially fair payment represent a transfer payment.

Study Sample

Data on the socioeconomic characteristics, 1972 OAI benefit level, and OAI benefit and claim status information for persons represented in the study sample were obtained from the 1973 Current Population Survey-Administrative Record Exact Match File. The 1973 Exact Match File unites survey records for persons included in the March 1973 Current Population Survey to their corresponding benefit and earnings information in the administrative records of the Social Security Administration and to specific items from their 1972 IRS individual income tax returns (Aziz, Kilss, and Scheuren, 1978; Kilss and Scheuren, 1978; Scheuren and Tyler, 1975). Additional earnings information was obtained from the Longitudinal Social Security Exact Match File, 1937–1976. This file includes longitudinal earnings data on adults represented in the 1973 Exact Match File. The study sample included 353 single persons aged 62 and older and 2,771 couples where at least one member was age 62 or older (the data set is described in detail in appendix 1). A record from the 1973 Exact Match File was included in the study sample if:[1] 1) the individual was 62 or older; 2) the individual retired between 1961 and 1973; 3) the individual represented a "good match";[2] 4) the claim code in 1972 indicated retired, special age-72 or transitional claim type; and 5) the beneficiary code in 1972 indicated worker-only or wife.

This study investigates the OAI program exclusively; hence, reported benefits include primary worker, spousal, transitional, and special age-72 benefits.[3] The level of primary worker benefits received by the worker-beneficiary is a function of the worker's average monthly earnings, age at retirement, and level of postretirement earnings. Spousal benefits are 50 percent of the retired worker's primary insurance amount adjusted for the spouse's retirement age and postretirement earnings. All of these benefit levels are automatically indexed to the consumer price index beginning in 1975.

Historical Contribution Base and Tax Rates

Covered workers and their respective employers are assessed a proportional payroll tax on earnings up to the annual maximum taxable limit.

In 1937, a combined employee-employer 2-percent payroll tax was assessed on the first $3,000. Both the contribution base and payroll tax rate have been periodically increased since 1937. By 1972, the combined tax rate was 9.2 percent applied to the first $9,000. The initial impact of the OAI payroll tax rate is shared equally by employees and employers; however, it is assumed that the final burden of the tax is borne by labor (i.e., that there is 100-percent backward shifting).[4]

The historical tax rate series employed in this study is based on the OAI tax rate series constructed by Leimer (1976). Leimer used a historical-net-expenditure-decomposition technique to divide past OASDI contributions along functional lines according to net expenditures on three separate and distinct Social Security programs: old-age, survivor, and disability. The OAI tax rate series was derived by allocating a share of the OASDI tax rate according to the proportion of total program expenditures accounted for by the OAI portion in every year. Expenditures on old-age insurance differ from survivor and disability insurance in that OAI represents savings for retirement, whereas SI and DI provide term insurance prior to retirement.[5]

Interest Rates

A low rate of return was selected in determining the compounded value of total OAI contributions. The annual yield on U.S. government bonds from 1937 to 1972 was used in the traditional compounding scheme. This low rate of return reflects the riskless nature of the retirement investment. An absence of risk is assumed since the government essentially guarantees the worker full repayment of OAI contributions upon retirement.

Survivor Probabilities

Three tables of survivor probabilities were used to calculate annuity counterfactuals. Survivor probabilities describe the statistical probability of a person life age x (say, 65) surviving to life age x + 1 (say, 66). The age-specific (gender-merged) and age-race-sex-specific tables are based on Social Security Administration (SSA) survivor probabilities for persons 62 and older and Vital Statistics Life Tables for persons younger than 62. The SSA probabilities were estimated using 1968–1969 Medicare data for persons who were either covered by Hospital Insurance or Supplemental Medical Insurance and at least 62 years old (Bayo, 1972; Myers and Bayo, 1965).

In addition, a table of survivor probabilities differentiated by age, race, sex, marital status, education, and income was used. The socioeconomic-adjusted survival probability table is based on tables constructed by Kitagawa and Hauser (1973) and modified by Leimer (1978).

Annuity Formulas

Burkhauser and Warlick (1981) estimated a transfer component (1972 OASI benefit level less the actuarially fair benefit level) from a life-cycle model using the 1973 Exact Match File. The actuarially fair counterfactual was an immediate whole life annuity payable on an annual basis.[6] Their work is extended in this study to account for the monthly disbursement of benefits and price indexing of benefits. The annuity is assumed to be purchased on the date of retirement with the retirement candidate's compounded OAI contributions. The first benefit payment from the actuarially fair retirement insurance is received at the end of the first month of the retirement period.

The variables used to calculate the formulas discussed in this section are as follows: PV^S = present value of a one-dollar nonindexed whole life annuity payable monthly; PV^C = present value of a one-dollar nonindexed joint-and-two-thirds whole life annuity payable monthly; PV^{S*} = present value of a one-dollar price-indexed whole life annuity payable monthly; PV^{C*} = present value of a one-dollar price-indexed joint-and-two-thirds whole life annuity payable monthly; R = male's age at retirement; $\overline{R}$ = female's age at retirement; ${}_{\overline{R}+t}S_{\overline{R}}$ = the probability of the annuitant surviving to life age $\overline{R} + t$, given she is already life age $\overline{R}$; $101-\overline{R}$ = number of years in the retirement period; i = nominal discount rate (5 percent); J = wife's age at husband's retirement; Z = husband's age at wife's retirement; s = deferment period $|K - Q|$; Q = retirement age difference between husband and wife $(R - \overline{R})$; K = age difference between husband and wife; c = expected growth in future prices;[7] i' = indexed discount rate (2.189 percent); and X = age of the oldest member of the couple at the end of the deferment period.

The retirement candidate purchases an actuarially fair life annuity with her total compounded OAI contributions (TC_i) on the date of retirement (RE). The present value of a one-dollar nonindexed life annuity payable 12 times a year purchased by a single person is

$$PV^S = \left\{ \sum_{t=1}^{101-\overline{R}} \frac{1}{(1+i)^t} \, {}_{\overline{R}+t}S_{\overline{R}} \right\} + \frac{11}{24}. \qquad (4.1)$$

The present value of a one-dollar nonindexed joint-and-two-thirds annuity payable 12 times a year purchased by each member of a couple on the date of retirement is [8]

$$\mathrm{PV^C} = \left[\frac{2}{3}\left\{\left(\underbrace{\sum_{t=1}^{101-R} \frac{1}{(1+i)^t}\,{}_{R+t}S_R}_{(a)}\right) + \frac{11}{24}\right\}\right.$$

$$+ \frac{2}{3}\left(\underbrace{\frac{1}{(1+i)^s}\,{}_{J+s}S_J}_{(b)}\left\{\left(\underbrace{\sum_{t=1}^{101-\overline{R}} \frac{1}{(1+i)^t}\,{}_{\overline{R}+t}S_{\overline{R}}}_{(c)}\right) + \frac{11}{24}\right\}\right)$$

$$\left. - \frac{1}{3}\left(\underbrace{\frac{1}{(1+i)^s}\,{}_{J+s}S_J \bullet {}_{R+s}S_R}_{(d)}\left\{\left(\underbrace{\sum_{t=1}^{101-X} \frac{1}{(1+i)^t}\,{}_{\overline{R}+t}S_{\overline{R}} \bullet {}_{Z+t}S_Z}_{(e)}\right) + \frac{11}{24}\right\}\right)\right]. \tag{4.2}$$

Term (a) in equation 4.2 is a restatement of equation 4.1 and states that the person purchasing the annuity will receive two-thirds of one if he lives. The second term states that the spouse will receive two-thirds of one when she is eligible for retirement (in the case where the husband is purchasing the annuity). Term (b) is the discount and survivorship factor capturing the deferment period for spousal benefits in the case where the spouse is younger than the husband and not of retirement age. The age difference between the husband and wife is equal to K years; the difference in their retirement ages, $R - \overline{R}$, equals Q where R = the husband's age at retirement and $\overline{R}$ = the spouse's retirement age. The length of deferment period equals s where $s = |K - Q|$. If K = 0 and Q = 0, then s = 0 and terms (b) and (c) collapse to $2/3\mathrm{PV^S}$—the annuity formula for a single person multiplied by two-thirds.

Term (e) in equation 4.2 is a joint life annuity. It defines group failure when the first member of the group dies or fails to qualify for benefit payments. Failure to qualify in this case means one of the members does not meet the OAI eligibility criteria. The joint life annuity pays only if both persons are alive *and* retired and provides payments for the duration of the shorter surviving status. Term (d) accounts for the time value of money and the compound probability of both members surviving the deferment period, s.

The price-indexed annuity formula guarantees payment of a real stream of income over the annuitant's retirement period. The nonindexed formulas discussed above are modified by a CPI expected growth factor and an adjusted interest rate.[9]

The present value of a one-dollar price-indexed life annuity payable 12 times a year purchased by a single person is

$$\mathrm{PV^{S*}} = \left\{\left(\frac{1}{(1+c)}\sum_{t=1}^{101-\overline{R}} \frac{1}{(1+i')^t}\,{}_{\overline{R}+t}S_{\overline{R}}\right) + \frac{11}{24}\right\}. \tag{4.3}$$

The present value of a one-dollar price-indexed joint-and-two-thirds life annuity payable 12 times per year purchased by each member of a couple is

$$PV^{C*} = \left[\frac{2}{3}\left\{\left(\frac{1}{(1+c)}\sum_{t=1}^{101-R}\frac{1}{(1+i')^t}\,{}_{R+t}S_R\right) + \frac{11}{24}\right\}\right.$$

$$+ \frac{2}{3}\left(\frac{1}{(1+i')^s}\,{}_{J+s}S_J\left\{\left(\frac{1}{(1+c)}\sum_{t=1}^{101-\bar{R}}\frac{1}{(1+i')^t}\,{}_{\bar{R}R+t}S_{\bar{R}}\right) + \frac{11}{24}\right\}\right)$$

$$- \frac{1}{3}\left(\frac{1}{(1+i')^s}\,{}_{J+s}S_J \cdot {}_{R+s}S_R\left\{\left(\frac{1}{(1+c)}\sum_{t=1}^{101-X}\frac{1}{(1+i')^t}\,{}_{\bar{R}+t}S_{\bar{R}}\right.\right.\right.$$

$$\left.\left.\left.\left. \cdot\, {}_{Z+t}S_Z\right) + \frac{11}{24}\right\}\right)\right]. \quad (4.4)$$

The price-indexed formulas state that the retirement candidate purchases a one-dollar life annuity and a series of staggered deferred life annuities paying increments of 1 + c. The nominal accretions in income each year will maintain the real purchasing power of one dollar over the individual's retirement period, assuming that the actual inflation rate equals the expected rate.

Annuity-Type Counterfactuals

There are six annuity-type counterfactuals estimated in this study. The counterfactuals are described in table 4.1. Annuity-type counterfactuals mimic the features of the OAI program and differ in terms of the survivor probability tables used and whether benefits are indexed or nonindexed. The value of the monthly annuity benefit is dependent on the accumulated value of OAI contributions, the extent of insurance protection, and the degree to which the insurer can tailor benefits to reflect differentials in survivorship.

Earnings Test

The annuity benefits were, in some cases, adjusted for the earnings test. The modeling of the earnings test reflects the legislated earnings test in 1972. Counterfactuals adjusted by the earnings test receive special mention in chapter 5.

A beneficiary's annuity benefit was adjusted by a reduction factor,

Table 4.1. Description of Annuity Counterfactuals

Annuity counterfactual	Characteristics
Type 1	Traditional compounding scheme, nonindexed formula, and gender-merged survivorship tables
Type 2	Traditional compounding scheme, nonindexed formula, and sex-race-distinct survivorship tables
Type 3	Traditional compounding scheme, nonindexed formula, and socioeconomic survivorship tables
Type 4	Traditional compounding scheme, indexed formula, and gender-merged survivorship tables
Type 5	Traditional compounding scheme, indexed formula, and sex-race-distinct survivorship tables
Type 6	Traditional compounding scheme, indexed formula, and socioeconomic survivorship tables

RED_i, if earnings in 1972 exceeded \$1,680. The reduction factor is calculated by

$$RED_i = 1/2(REP72_i - 1{,}680) \tag{4.5}$$

if $REP72_i \leqslant 2{,}880$; or

$$RED_i = 600 + (REP72_i - 2{,}880) \tag{4.6}$$

if $REP72_i > 2{,}880$. $REP72_i$ represents beneficiary i's 1972 reported earnings.

Redistribution Components

The counterfactuals described above were used to calculate the redistribution components, RC_i. The redistribution components determine the portion of the beneficiary's 1972 Social Security benefits that she did not pay for with her lifetime OAI contributions.

For single beneficiaries, the redistribution components were calculated by the following:

$$RC_{ij} = b_{oi} = b_{ij} \quad \text{for } j = 1, 2, 3 \tag{4.7}$$

and

$$RC^{*}_{ij} = b_{oi} - b^{*}_{ij} \quad \text{for } j = 4, 5, 6 \tag{4.8}$$

where RC_{ij} and RC^{*}_{ij} = beneficiary i's redistribution component for annuity-type j; b_{oi} = 1972 OAI benefit level for beneficiary i; b_{ij} = nonindexed annuity-type j benefit level for beneficiary i; and b^{*}_{ij} = indexed annuity-type j benefit level for beneficiary i.

The redistribution component calculations for married persons are similar to the components calculated for single persons but require the inclusion of both the husband and wife's annuity-type benefit. Family annuity benefits from the joint-and-two-thirds annuity were assumed to be equally owned by the husband and wife, an assumption that has important implications in terms of the relative share of redistribution received by men and women in different household types.

If the husband and wife are retired, then the redistribution components for each member of the couple are calculated by

$$RC_{ij} = b_{oi} - 0.5(b_{ij} + {}_{-}b_{ij}) \quad \text{for } j = 1, 2, 3; \tag{4.9}$$

$${}_{-}RC_{ij} = {}_{-}b_{oi} - 0.5(b_{ij} + {}_{-}b_{ij}) \quad \text{for } j = 1, 2, 3; \tag{4.10}$$

$$RC^{*}_{ij} = b_{oi} - 0.5(b^{*}_{ij} + {}_{-}b^{*}_{ij}) \quad \text{for } j = 4, 5, 6; \tag{4.11}$$

$${}_{-}RC^{*}_{ij} = {}_{-}b_{oi} - 0.5(b^{*}_{ij} + {}_{-}b^{*}_{ij}) \quad \text{for } j = 4, 5, 6; \tag{4.12}$$

where b_{oi} = female's 1972 OAI benefit; ${}_{-}b_{o}$ = male's 1972 OAI benefit; b_{ij} = female i's nonindexed annuity-type j benefit level; ${}_{-}b_{ij}$ = male i's nonindexed annuity-type j benefit level; b^{*}_{ij} = female i's indexed annuity-type j benefit level; and ${}_{-}b^{*}_{ij}$ = male i's indexed annuity-type j benefit level. If only one member of the couple is retired, then the redistribution calculations are identical to those calculated for single persons.

Behavioral Responses

The removal of the worker-financed retirement insurance was accomplished by estimating a series of worker-specific, actuarially fair counterfactuals assuming no behavioral responses. That is, it was assumed that worker participants would not respond by altering their labor or savings decisions when retirement benefits were calculated using strictly insurance benefit formulas as compared to the OAI retirement benefit formula. An actuarially fair retirement system was used only as a counterfactual to determine the retirement benefits the worker-beneficiary actually paid for through OAI contributions after contributions were already paid into the system. This annuity-type counterfactual was then used to isolate the size of the benefits the beneficiary received from the social adequacy function of the government's retirement program. The benefit disentanglement was undertaken with the sole intention of assessing the benefit incidence of the transfers received by the 1972 retirement cohort from the current working population. The incidence was examined to isolate the effects of socioeconomic characteristics on the direction and size of the transfers and to ensure that the intent of the law was consistent with the overall effect of the program.

The ex post annuity calculations and comparisons used in this study are confined to the narrow disentanglement interpretation discussed above. They cannot be accurately interpreted to reflect the effect of a program switch from the current OAI program to an actuarially fair retirement system. Empirical results, to date, show that the Social Security program does affect labor supply and savings decisions (Boskin, 1977; Burkhauser, 1980; Burkhauser and Quinn, 1981; Feldstein, 1974; Pellechio, 1978).[10] In addition, research by Browning (1975) and Burkhauser and Turner (1978 and 1983) indicates that an actuarially fair retirement system would have significant labor supply implications across the life cycle.

In light of existing empirical research on the economic effects of the Social Security program, a study on the privitization of the program would necessitate ex ante modeling of an actuarially fair retirement system that would fully incorporate behavioral responses by worker participants. At best, this study only approximates the effects of a privitization of the Social Security program.

5

New Annuity-Welfare Model Descriptive Results

The Benefit Incidence of the 1972 Old-Age Insurance Program: All Households

Table 5.1 displays the estimated benefit incidence of the OAI program in 1972 for the 1962–1972 retirement cohorts based on type-6 annuity counterfactuals. In the aggregate, $7.09 million in OAI benefits were paid to retired beneficiaries in this subsample; approximately 89 percent of the benefits received were transfers from the current working generation. The $6.3 million in intergenerational transfers were not, however, evenly distributed across the income groups. Contrary to the social adequacy objective, the low-income groups ($0–3,000) represented 15 percent of the sample and received 10 percent of the intergenerational transfers, whereas the middle-income groups ($3,000–8,000) received 57 percent of the transfers but represented 53 percent of the sample. The high-income groups ($8,001 plus) received 33 percent of the transfers but included 32 percent of the sample. In absolute terms, the middle-income groups received the largest share of the intergenerational transfers.

The extent of the intracohort redistribution may be inferred from the absolute and relative size of the redistribution component across family income classes. Column 3 in table 5.1 indicates that all income groups received more than their money's worth from the Social Security program, since for each income class, the mean OAI benefit level (column 1) is larger than the actuarially fair benefit level (column 2). However, the largest relative gains were realized by low-income families. On average, the lowest income family group received $698 annually from OAI, of which $681, or 97.6 percent, was a result of the social adequacy feature of the program. Column 4 shows that the redistribution component, as a percentage of the mean OAI benefit level in 1972, generally decreased as the family income level in 1972 increased. This general pattern suggests that

Table 5.1. Benefit Incidence of the 1972 Old-Age Insurance Program

Total family income in 1972[a]	(1) OAI benefit level in 1972 (mean)	(2) Type-6 actuarially fair benefit, earnings-adjusted (mean)[b]	Redistribution component (3) Absolute difference (1)-(2)	Redistribution component (4) Percentage difference $\frac{(1)-(2)}{(1)} \times 100$	Household population distribution (in percents)
$ 0- 1,000	698	17	681	97.6	1
1,001- 1,500	1,065	76	989	92.9	1
1,501- 2,000	1,369	119	1,250	91.3	3
2,001- 2,500	1,618	141	1,477	91.3	5
2,501- 3,000	1,847	173	1,674	90.6	5
3,001- 3,500	2,071	220	1,851	89.4	6
3,501- 4,000	2,275	258	2,017	88.7	8
4,001- 5,000	2,499	287	2,212	88.5	13
5,001- 6,000	2,571	312	2,259	87.9	11
6,001- 8,000	2,517	312	2,205	87.6	15
8,001-10,000	2,381	281	2,100	88.2	9
10,001-20,000	2,271	240	2,031	89.4	18
20,001+	2,425	260	2,165	89.3	5
Total	$7.09[c]	$.796[c]	$6.294[c]	88.8	3,124
Mean	$2,283	$256	$2,027	88.8	

[a]Total family income includes OAI benefits in 1972.

[b]Annuity counterfactual based on the traditional compounding scheme, an indexed annuity formula, and socioeconomic survivorship tables.

[c]In millions of dollars.

the progressive benefit formula and minimum benefit provisions effectively redistributed income in favor of low-income households; that is, the program in 1972 was progressive.

There are several approaches that could be used to assess the overall progressivity of the OAI program. One approach is based on end-point comparisons. That is, the percentage of redistribution for the lowest income group is compared to the comparable measure for the highest income group. The relatively small low-to-high differential, 97.6 to 89.3 in column 4, suggests that the redistribution formula in 1972 was mildly progressive. Another approach evaluates progressivity in terms of a steadily falling percentage of redistribution as the income level increases. Note that the redistribution measure in column 4 of table 5.1 falls steadily as income rises (with the exception of $2,001–2,500) to the $8,001–10,000 group, after which the percentage of redistribution generally increases. The falling pattern for nine out of 13 income groups would, again, suggest that the program was generally progressive.

An alternative approach is to evaluate the program's overall progressivity by comparing the highest income group's percentage of redistribution to the percentage of redistribution for all other family income categories. A truly progressive program would have a steadily falling, positive differential as income increases, whereas a truly regressive program would have a steadily falling, negative differential as income increases. This type of comparison of the results presented in column 4 is displayed in figure 5.1, curve 1. Clearly, the OAI program demonstrated truly progressive features at income levels less than $3,501, but it displayed regressive, although not truly regressive, features at income levels greater than $3,500 but less than $10,001.

The different approaches used to assess progressivity can lead to different program assessments from the same descriptive statistics. The end-point approach indicates that the OAI program in 1972 was mildly progressive, whereas the patterned approach shows it to be generally progressive throughout the income classifications. However, the high-income-group-comparison approach shows that the program exhibited classic progressive features for low-income groups only and strong regressive features for all other income groups except the penultimate income group. These different approaches, when taken separately, can result in misleading and over-optimistic program performance assessment but, when taken together, can render a complete picture of the program's overall performance. That is, the OAI program in 1972 was mildly and generally progressive across income groups. But it also exhibited regressive features, resulting in lower relative returns to middle-income beneficiaries. Therefore, the intracohort transfer mechanism operated to pay the highest rel-

Figure 5.1. Progressivity of the OAI Program Using Socioeconomic-Adjusted Annuity Benefits Controlling for Earnings Test and Indexing

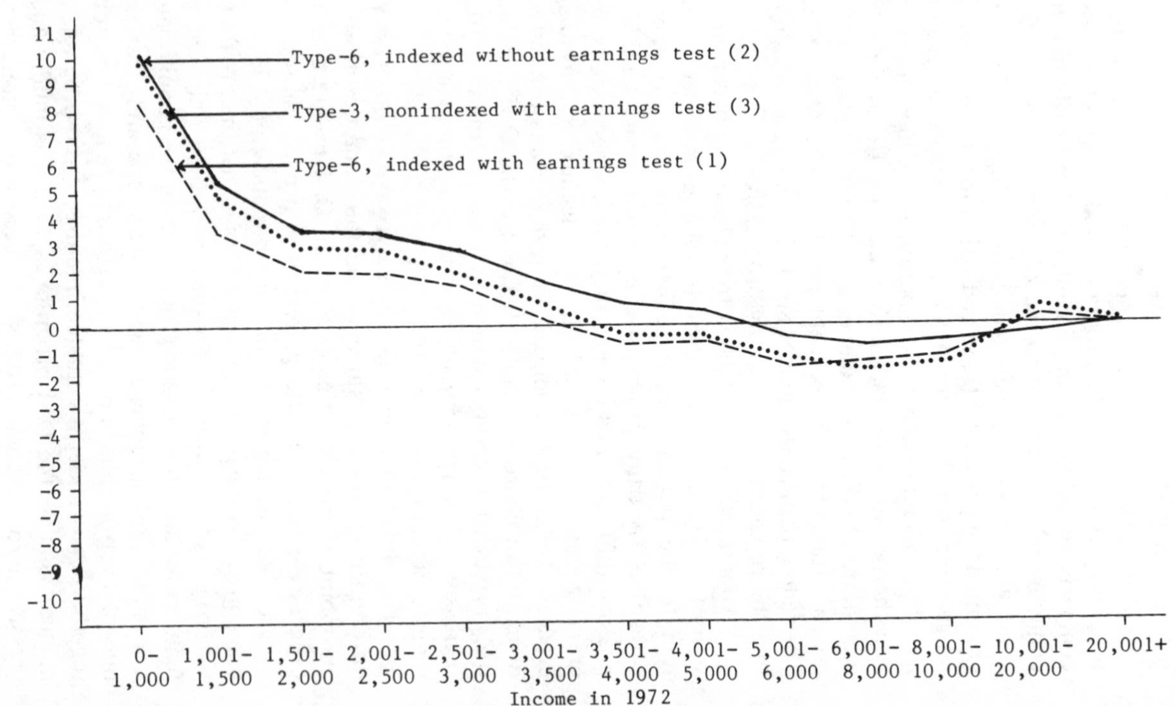

ative return to the low-income beneficiaries and the lowest relative returns to middle-income beneficiaries, which, in spite of being mildly and generally progressive, is inconsistent with the program's overall objective.

While the benefit formula and the minimum benefit provisions strongly influenced the pattern of the redistribution components, there are other confounding program features that exert an influence on the redistribution design, such as the earnings test, cost-of-living adjustments, and life contingencies. Table 5.2 isolates the effects of the earnings test and cost-of-living features on the percentage of redistribution across income groups. The life contingency influence is examined in Table 5.3.

The earnings test effect is presented in column 3 of table 5.2,[1] which measures the change in the percentage of redistribution when the earnings test is introduced into the program's design. Note that the earnings test does not affect the three lowest income groups, but it becomes an increasingly important influence on the estimated percentage of redistribution as family income level increases. The earnings test effect has its greatest impact on high-income families ($6,000 plus), which places upward pressure on their summary redistribution measures because their annuity benefits are reduced by the earnings test formula. The earnings test effect on the high-income-group-comparison approach to progressivity assessment can be seen by comparing curve 2 to curve 1 in figure 5.1. In the absence of the earnings test, the program was progressive at income levels less than $5,001 and regressive at income levels in excess of $5,000. The earnings test feature shifts the performance curve downward, introducing additional regressive features into the program's modus operandi.

Column 5 in table 5.2 isolates the change in the redistribution measure as a result of introducing price indexing into the program's design. Note that the absolute size of the redistribution measure increases for all income groups when inflation protection is included in the annuity counterfactual, ceteris paribus. This result is expected, at least initially, since the indexed annuity benefit is smaller than a nonindexed annuity benefit.[2] This is because the annuitant is insured against the risk of economic insecurity *and* inflation over an uncertain retirement period.

Although all income groups realized extra redistribution per dollar of OAI benefit when indexing was included in the program, the greatest relative gains were realized by high-income groups because of their longer life expectancies on average. Price indexing, when taken alone, did not alter progressivity conclusions, but it did generally reduce the level of progressivity at income levels less than $3,501 and slightly increased regressivity at income levels between $3,500 and $5,000 (see figure 5.1, curves 3 and 1).

The sensitivity of the progressivity conclusions to the survivorship

Table 5.2. Effect of the Earnings Test and Cost-of-Living Indexing on the Distribution of Redistribution (Expressed in Percentage Terms) for Socioeconomic-Adjusted Annuity Benefits[a]

Total family income in 1972[c]	Percentage of redistribution[b]				
	(1) Indexed and earnings-adjusted	(2) Indexed without earnings adjustment	(3) Change in redistribution (1)-(2)	(4) Nonindexed and earnings-adjusted	(5) Change in redistribution (1)-(4)
$ 0- 1,000	97.6	97.6	0.0	97.3	0.3
1,001- 1,500	92.9	92.9	0.0	92.5	0.4
1,501- 2,000	91.3	91.3	0.0	90.4	0.9
2,001- 2,500	91.3	91.1	0.2	90.4	0.9
2,501- 3,000	90.6	90.3	0.3	89.5	1.1
3,001- 3,500	89.4	89.1	0.3	88.2	1.2
3,501- 4,000	88.7	88.4	0.3	87.4	1.3
4,001- 5,000	88.5	88.2	0.3	87.0	1.5
5,001- 6,000	87.9	87.5	0.4	86.3	1.6
6,001- 8,000	87.6	86.8	0.8	85.8	1.8
8,001-10,000	88.2	87.1	1.1	86.3	1.9
10,001-20,000	89.4	87.6	1.8	87.8	1.6
20,001+	89.3	87.7	1.6	87.6	1.7
Mean	88.8	88.0	0.8	87.2	1.6

[a]All annuity benefits were calculated using socioeconomic-adjusted survivorship probabilities.

[b]Percentage of redistribution was calculated by taking the difference between the mean OAI benefit level in 1972 and the mean actuarially fair benefit level for an income class divided by the mean OAI benefit level in 1972.

[c]Total family income includes OAI benefits received in 1972.

Table 5.3. Changes in the Percentage of Redistribution under Different Survivorship Probability Assumptions

Total family income in 1972	Earnings-test-adjusted				
	Annuity-type, indexed			(4)	(5)
	(1) Type-4[a]	(2) Type-5[a]	(3) Type-6[a]	Change in percentage of redistribution (2)-(1)	(3)-(1)
$ 0- 1,000	97.7	97.8	97.6	0.1	-0.1
1,001- 1,500	93.9	94.1	92.9	0.2	-1.0
1,501- 2,000	91.8	92.0	91.3	0.2	-0.5
2,001- 2,500	91.3	91.6	91.3	0.3	0.0
2,501- 3,000	90.6	91.0	90.6	0.4	0.0
3,001- 3,500	89.4	89.7	89.4	0.3	0.0
3,501- 4,000	88.6	88.9	88.7	0.3	0.1
4,001- 5,000	88.2	88.6	88.5	0.4	0.3
5,001- 6,000	87.5	87.9	87.9	0.4	0.4
6,001- 8,000	87.1	87.5	87.6	0.4	0.5
8,001-10,000	87.7	88.1	88.2	0.4	0.5
10,001-20,000	88.9	89.3	89.4	0.4	0.5
20,001+	88.6	88.9	89.3	0.3	0.7
Mean	88.5	88.8	88.8	0.3	0.3

[a]Raw data used to calculate the percentage of distribution for each family income classification are available upon request.

probability assumption is examined in table 5.3. The benefit incidence for type-4, type-5, and type-6 counterfactuals is presented in columns 1, 2, and 3, respectively. Column 4 shows the change in the percentage of redistribution if the program adopted a sex-race-age discriminating policy as opposed to an age-only discriminating policy. The adoption of a sex-race-age discriminating policy resulted in an average gain of 0.3 cents of redistribution per dollar of OAI benefit. However, the adoption of a sex-race-age-education-income-marital status discriminating policy in place of an age-only policy (column 5) resulted in a marginal gain in redistribution for households with income levels in excess of $3,500, where the marginal gain generally increased as family income increased. The lowest income groups (0–2,000), on the other hand, realized a net loss in redistribution per dollar of OAI benefit. The marginal gain-loss observation is explained by the effect of income and education levels on longevity. That is, ceteris paribus, annuity benefits are higher (lower) for low (high) income earners because the probability of survival is positively related to income and education.

Contrary to Aaron's study (1977), the effects of socioeconomic differentials in survivorship do not reverse the direction of redistribution; instead, they "dampen" the extent of redistribution at the low end of the income scale and "elevate" the extent of redistribution at the high end of the income scale (consistent with Okonkwo's findings). The program's overall progressivity was virtually invariant to the use of gender-merged or sex-race-distinct survivorship rates (see curves 2 and 3 in figure 5.2). However, the use of socioeconomic-adjusted survivorship probabilities did augment the regressive features and attentuate the progressive features relative to less discriminating probabilities.

Basic summary statistics for counterfactuals one through six are presented in tables 5.4 and 5.5. The total and mean annuity benefit received in 1972 and the mean percentage of redistribution, controlling for survivorship assumption, indexing, and earnings test, are presented in table 5.4. The end-point summary statistics for all counterfactuals are shown in table 5.5. Note that the largest progressivity gap (12.2) resulted from a program characterized by age-only discrimination without an earnings penalty test or inflation protection. The smallest progressivity gap (8.3) resulted from a program that provided inflation protection, garnished a fraction of benefits for excessive postretirement earnings, and tapered benefits to reflect socioeconomic differentials in mortality.

The Effect of Differential Life Expectancies of Males and Females on the Benefit Incidence for Fully Insured Beneficiaries

Single Beneficiaries

Tables 5.6 and 5.7 show the effects of differential life expectancies of females and males on the benefit incidence for fully insured single beneficiaries. Type-4 annuity benefits were calculated employing gender-merged survivorship rates, whereas type-5 benefits were calculated using sex-race-distinct rates. All contribution classes, independent of sex and annuity type, received positive transfers from the OAI program (i.e., the mean OAI benefit level exceeded the annuity-type benefit level). However, the absolute size of the transfer depended on sex and annuity type. Male

Figure 5.2. Progressivity of the OAI Program Using Different Survival Probability Assumptions

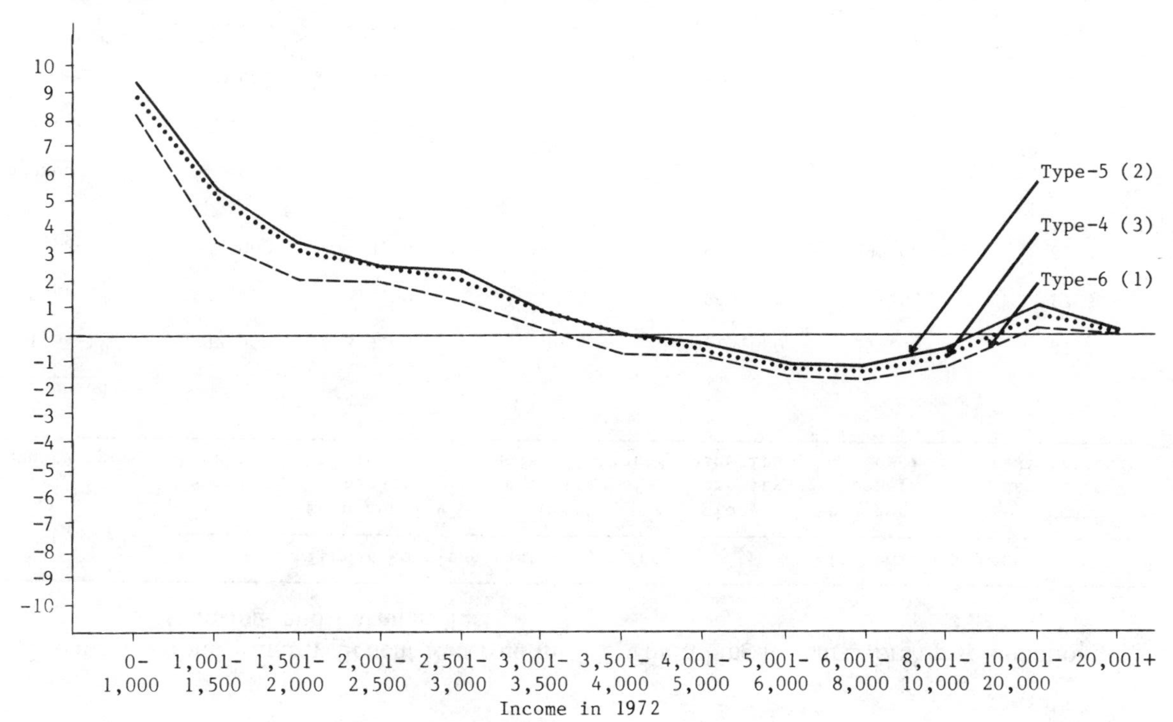

Table 5.4. Total Annuity Benefit Received in 1972 Controlling for Survivorship Assumption, Indexing, and Earnings Test

	Without earnings test			With earnings test		
Annuity type	Total annuity benefits	Mean annuity benefit level	Mean[a] percentage of redistribution	Total annuity benefits	Mean annuity benefit level	Mean[a] percentage of redistribution
Nonindexed						
Type-1[b]	$992,000	319.00	86.0	$925,000	298.00	87.0
Type-2[c]	971,000	313.00	86.3	905,000	291.00	87.3
Type-3[d]	972,000	313.00	86.3	906,000	292.00	87.2
Indexed						
Type-4[b]	877,000	282.00	87.6	820,000	264.00	88.5
Type-5[c]	850,000	274.00	88.0	794,000	256.00	88.8
Type-6[d]	852,000	274.00	88.0	796,000	256.00	88.8

[a]Total benefits minus total annuity benefits divided by total benefits.

[b]Calculations based on gender-merged survivor probabilities.

[c]Calculations based on sex-race-distinct survivor probabilities.

[d]Calculations based on socioeconomic-adjusted survivor probabilities.

Table 5.5. Percentage-Point Gap between Poorest and Richest Income Groups

Survivor probability assumption	Without earnings test				With earnings test			
	Nonindexed		Indexed		Nonindexed		Indexed	
	Poorest to richest	Second poorest to richest	Poorest to richest	Second poorest to richest	Poorest to richest	Second poorest to richest	Poorest to richest	Second poorest to richest
Gender-merged	12.2	7.9	10.7	6.9	10.3	6.0	9.1	5.3
Sex-race-distinct	12.1	7.9	10.4	6.7	10.2	6.0	8.9	5.2
Socioeconomic	11.6	6.8	9.9	5.2	9.7	4.9	8.3	3.6

beneficiaries received smaller annuity benefits when gender-merged rates were employed relative to a program using sex-distinct rates, ceteris paribus. This observed relationship is expected, since sex-distinct rates adjust benefit levels upward for the relatively shorter life expectancies of men as a group vis-à-vis women as a group. On the other hand, female beneficiaries received larger annuity benefits (hence, smaller redistribution components) when gender-merged rates were used relative to sex-distinct rates. Again, this is an expected result, since sex-distinct rates adjust benefit levels downward for the relatively longer life expectancies of women as a group.

The annuity benefit differentials for female and male beneficiaries are shown in column 3 in tables 5.6 and 5.7, respectively. The negative differentials for female beneficiaries and the positive differentials for male beneficiaries indicate that single women as a group are made differentially better off in a retirement program that does not sex discriminate benefit levels to account for the women's longer life expectancies relative to men's. Single female beneficiaries as a group received annuity benefits that were approximately 16 percent higher in a gender-merged retirement system relative to a sex-race discriminating system, whereas their male counterparts as a group received benefits that were approximately 7 percent lower. Hence, in a sex-neutral retirement program, single male beneficiaries received lower benefit levels than they would in a sex discriminating program, which compensated for the slightly higher benefit levels paid to single female beneficiaries.

A similar comparison can be made between type-5 and type-6 annuity counterfactuals. Column 6 in tables 5.6 and 5.7 show that single persons, in general, received marginal accretions in their annuity benefits when the effects of marital status, education, and income levels are incorporated into their life contingencies. These other socioeconomic variables affecting longevity tend to offset the effect of the sex variable for single women and reinforce the effect of the sex variable for single men. The overall benefit differential resulting from the incorporation of sex, race, marital status, education, and income variables into annuity benefit calculations is presented in column 7 of tables 5.6 and 5.7. Single female beneficiaries received annuity benefits that were approximately 8 percent lower in a socioeconomic discriminating program relative to an age-only discriminating program, whereas single male beneficiaries received annuity benefits that were approximately 30 percent higher.

Married Beneficiaries

Tables 5.8 and 5.9 show the effect of differential life expectancies of females and males on the benefit incidence for fully insured married ben-

Table 5.6. Effect of Differential Life Expectancies of Females on Benefit Incidence for Single Workers Controlling for Total OAI Contributions[a]

Total OAI[e] contributions in 1972 dollars	(1) Type-4[b] actu-arially fair benefit	(2) Type-5[c] actu-arially fair benefit	(3) Benefit differ-ential (2)-(1)	(4) Type-5 actu-arially fair benefit	(5) Type-6[d] actu-arially fair benefit	(6) Benefit differ-ential (5)-(4)	(7) Overall benefit differ-ential (5)-(1)	Population
$ 500<	22	19	-3	19	21	2	-1	17
501-1,000	62	54	-8	54	62	8	0	15
1,001-1,500	94	81	-13	81	87	6	-7	13
1,501-2,000	142	122	-20	122	130	8	-12	12
2,001-2,500	183	158	-25	158	173	15	-10	15
2,501-3,000	211	182	-29	182	198	16	-13	15
3,001-3,500	229	197	-32	197	216	19	-13	12
3,501-4,000	293	252	-41	252	277	25	-16	13
4,001-4,500	350	301	-49	301	320	19	-30	17
4,501-5,000	402	346	-56	346	378	32	-24	7
5,001-6,000	410	351	-59	351	364	13	-46	36
6,001-7,000	492	421	-71	421	456	35	-36	12
7,001-8,000	544	466	-78	466	506	40	-38	9
8,001-9,000	767	660	-107	660	697	37	-70	6
9,001+	626	537	-89	537	562	25	-64	8
Total	$59,764	$51,355	-$8,409	$51,355	$54,853	$3,498	-$4,911	207

[a]Female beneficiaries are defined as single female retirees who are fully insured and collecting primary benefits in 1972.

[b]Type-4 indexed annuity estimates are based on gender-merged survivor probabilities, unadjusted.

[c]Type-5 indexed annuity estimates are based on sex-race-distinct survivor probabilities, unadjusted.

[d]Type-6 indexed annuity estimates are based on socioeconomic-adjusted survivor probabilities, unadjusted.

[e]The 1972 dollar value of OAI contributions paid by the worker over her work history. The OAI contributions were accumulated assuming that there was 100-percent backward shifting of the OAI tax rate and compounding at U.S. government bond interest rates.

Table 5.7. Effect of Differential Life Expectancies of Males on Benefit Incidence for Single Workers Controlling for Total OAI Contributions[a]

Total OAI[e] contributions in 1972 dollars	(1) Type-4[b] actu-arially fair benefit	(2) Type-5[c] actu-arially fair benefit	(3) Benefit differ-ential (2)-(1)	(4) Type-5 actu-arially fair benefit	(5) Type-6[d] actu-arially fair benefit	(6) Benefit differ-ential (5)-(4)	(7) Overall benefit differ-ential (5)-(1)	Population
$ 500<	23	25	2	25	29	4	6	10
501-1,000	61	66	5	66	78	12	17	10
1,001-1,500	91	99	8	99	119	20	28	17
1,501-2,000	82	88	6	88	104	16	22	4
2,001-2,500	172	187	15	187	240	53	68	6
2,501-3,000	215	233	18	233	287	54	72	7
3,001-3,500	263	284	21	284	347	63	84	11
3,501-4,000	302	326	24	326	389	63	87	5
4,001-4,500	313	337	24	337	401	64	88	7
4,501-5,000	369	399	30	399	484	85	115	7
5,001-6,000	426	461	35	461	556	95	130	11
6,001-7,000	469	505	36	505	595	90	126	10
7,001-8,000	521	561	40	561	664	103	143	11
8,001-9,000	677	731	54	731	857	126	180	4
9,001+	827	899	72	899	1,100	201	273	6
Total	$37,157	$40,131	$2,974	$40,131	$48,207	$8,076	$11,050	126

[a]Male beneficiaries are defined as single male retirees who are fully insured and collecting primary benefits in 1972.

[b]Type-4 indexed annuity estimates are based on gender-merged survivor probabilities, unadjusted.

[c]Type-5 indexed annuity estimates are based on sex-race-distinct survivor probabilities, unadjusted.

[d]Type-6 indexed annuity estimates are based on socioeconomic-adjusted survivor probabilities, unadjusted.

[e]The 1972 dollar value of OAI contributions paid by the worker over his work history. The OAI contributions were accumulated assuming that there was 100-percent backward shifting of the OAI tax rate and compounding at U.S. government bond interest rates.

eficiaries. The cross-subsidization by sex found in the case for single beneficiaries was not observed when the annuity benefit comparisons were made across married persons. Actuarially fair benefit levels for married persons were approximately 3 percent higher, independent of the sex of the primary annuitant, in a retirement system that did not sex discriminate relative to a sex discriminating program (see column 3 of tables 5.8 and 5.9). First, note that *both* the male and female received annuity benefits that were 3 percent higher in a sex-neutral retirement program. Within a married household, the effects of sex differentials are neutralized because the joint-and-two-thirds annuity insures the male *and* female members of the couple. The absolute size of the annuity benefit received is invariant to the sex of the annuitant who actually purchases the annuity in either program type.

Second, the sex-neutral bias in favor of married persons as a group is a result of the joint-and-two-thirds annuity, which insures the life of the shorter-lived (on average) male, the longer-lived female, and the longest-lived survivor, who is typically female. The surviving wife will, in a sex-neutral system, receive artificially high benefit levels for the duration of widowhood. The relatively higher benefit levels for married households in a sex-neutral, actuarially fair retirement program are financed primarily by single, male beneficiaries who receive smaller annuity benefits because of the assumption of identical life contingencies for males and females.

The effect of incorporating other socioeconomic variables can be seen in column 6 of tables 5.8 and 5.9. Education, income, and marital status effects tend to further reduce the size of the annuity benefit received by married persons. Specifically, annuity benefits are approximately 1.3 percent lower in a socioeconomic discriminating program relative to a sex-race discriminating program. Again, this is expected, since married persons tend to have a longer life expectancy relative to their nonmarried counterparts. The overall benefit differential is represented in column 7 of tables 5.8 and 5.9. Generally speaking, married persons, independent of sex, received benefits that were approximately 4 percent lower in a socioeconomic discriminating program relative to an age-only discriminating program.

The Effect of Retirement Year on the Benefit Incidence of Single Workers Only

The effect of retirement year on the percentage of redistribution is shown in table 5.10. The retirement year is divided into three categories: 1962–1965, 1966–1969, and 1970–1972. The results are shown for type-3 and type-6 annuity counterfactuals and displayed by total family income

Table 5.8. Effect of Differential Life Expectancies of Females on Benefit Incidence for Married Workers Controlling for Total OAI Contributions: Females Only

Total OAI contributions in 1972 dollars[a,b]	(1) Type-4 actu-arially fair benefit[c]	(2) Type-5 actu-arially fair benefit[d]	(3) Benefit differ-ential (2)-(1)	(4) Type-5 actu-arially fair benefit	(5) Type-6 actu-arially fair benefit[e]	(6) Benefit differ-ential (5)-(4)	(7) Overall benefit differ-ential (5)-(1)	Population
$ 500<	21	20	-1	20	20	0	-1	132
501-1,000	50	48	-2	48	48	0	-2	130
1,001-1,500	83	80	-3	80	80	0	-3	97
1,501-2,000	110	107	-3	107	105	-2	-5	89
2,001-2,500	145	141	-4	141	140	-1	-5	82
2,501-3,000	172	166	-6	166	165	-1	-7	59
3,001-3,500	204	198	-6	198	194	-4	-10	51
3,501-4,000	242	234	-8	234	231	-3	-11	45
4,001-4,500	275	268	-7	268	263	-5	-12	41
4,501-5,000	341	329	-12	329	324	-5	-17	23
5,001-6,000	358	346	-12	346	341	-5	-17	40
6,001-7,000	360	348	-12	348	338	-10	-22	26
7,001-8,000	452	441	-11	441	435	-6	-17	17
8,001-9,000	449	436	-13	436	426	-10	-23	10
9,001+	479	458	-21	458	441	-17	-38	5
Total	$127,919	$123,835	-$4,084	$123,835	$122,094	-$1,741	-$5,825	847

[a]Female beneficiaries are defined as married female retirees who are fully insured and collecting primary benefits in 1972.

[b]The 1972 dollar value of OAI contributions paid by the worker over her work history. The OAI contributions were accumulated assuming that there was 100-percent backward shifting of the OAI tax rate and compounding at U.S. government bond interest rates.

[c]Type-4 indexed annuity estimates are based on gender-merged survivor probabilities, unadjusted.

[d]Type-5 indexed annuity estimates are based on sex-race-distinct survivor probabilities, unadjusted.

[e]Type-6 indexed annuity estimates are based on socioeconomic-adjusted survivor probabilities, unadjusted.

Table 5.9. Effect of Differential Life Expectancies of Males on Benefit Incidence for Married Workers Controlling for Total OAI Contributions: Males Only

Total OAI contributions in 1972 dollars[a,b]	(1) Type-4 actu-arially fair benefit[c]	(2) Type-5 actu-arially fair benefit[d]	(3) Benefit differ-ential (2)-(1)	(4) Type-5 actu-arially fair benefit	(5) Type-6 actu-arially fair benefit[e]	(6) Benefit differ-ential (5)-(4)	(7) Overall benefit differ-ential (5)-(1)	Population
$ 500<	20	19	-1	19	18	-1	-2	104
501-1,000	46	45	-1	45	45	0	-1	156
1,001-1,500	78	75	-3	75	75	0	-3	134
1,501-2,000	109	106	-3	106	105	-1	-4	133
2,001-2,500	130	126	-4	126	125	-1	-5	129
2,501-3,000	173	168	-5	168	166	-2	-7	138
3,001-3,500	209	203	-6	203	200	-3	-9	125
3,501-4,000	234	227	-7	227	226	-1	-8	143
4,001-4,500	264	256	-8	256	254	-2	-10	133
4,501-5,000	289	280	-9	280	277	-3	-12	131
5,001-6,000	330	321	-9	321	318	-3	-12	229
6,001-7,000	406	395	-11	395	389	-6	-17	214
7,001-8,000	433	421	-12	421	416	-5	-17	171
8,001-9,000	478	465	-13	465	460	-5	-18	176
9,001+	483	469	-14	469	462	-7	-21	247
Total	$647,180	$629,418	-$17,762	$629,418	$621,542	-$7,876	-$25,638	2,363

[a]Male beneficiaries are defined as married male retirees who are fully insured and collecting primary benefits in 1972.

[b]The 1972 dollar value of OAI contributions paid by the worker over his work history. The OAI contributions were accumulated assuming that there was 100-percent backward shifting of the OAI tax rate and compounding at U.S. government bond interest rates.

[c]Type-4 indexed annuity estimates are based on gender-merged survivor probabilities, unadjusted.

[d]Type-5 indexed annuity estimates are based on sex-race-distinct survivor probabilities, unadjusted.

[e]Type-6 indexed annuity estimates are based on socioeconomic-adjusted survivor probabilities, unadjusted.

classifications. Except in a few cases (notably, when the cell size is small), the percentage of redistribution falls as the retirement year increases, holding family income constant. Also, the percentage of redistribution is quite stable for the lowest income group, which is consistent with the minimum benefit provision. The generally observed inverse relationship between the percentage of redistribution and the date of retirement supports the findings of Parsons and Munro (1977), Freiden, Leimer, and Hoffman (1976), Burkhauser and Warlick (1981), and Pellechio and Goodfellow (1983). The general decline in the redistribution measure reflects the maturing of the program.

The Benefit Incidence of the 1972 Old-Age Insurance Program: Married, Both-Retired Households Only

The Effect of the Wife's Work Status on Benefit Incidence

There are 1,394 couples included in this sample: 614 two-earner couples and 780 one-earner couples. See table 5.11 for a description of the married, *both*-retired data set. The effect of the wife's work status on the distributional impact of the OAI program is examined in tables 5.12 and 5.13. Female beneficiaries were classified by their work status (work status was determined by OAI beneficiary eligibility criteria) and household income in 1972. Table 5.12 is similar to table 5.1 except that only married households in which both the husband and wife were retired in 1972 are included in the data set.

Similar to the results in table 5.1, all female beneficiaries, independent of work status and family income level, received positive income transfers from the OAI program in 1972 (that is, the redistribution components in columns 4a and 8a of table 5.12 are positive). The redistribution component expressed as a percentage of the female's OAI benefit level is negatively related to family income below $5,001.

Table 5.13 compares the differences in OAI benefit level (column 1), yearly annuity benefit in a type-6 actuarially fair retirement system based on the actual contributions made by the female (column 2) and the male (column 3), and the redistribution components in percentage terms (column 4) for working and nonworking women across family income categories. The working woman who qualifies for benefits on her own account received, on average, retirement benefits that were approximately 50 percent larger than the dependents benefits received by the nonworking woman. The benefit differential ranges from 21 percent for the lowest income category to 69 percent for the highest income category.[3]

Table 5.10. Effect of Retirement Year on Benefit Incidence for Single Workers

Total family income in 1972	Type-3, nonindexed[a]			Type-6, indexed[a]			Population		
	Redistribution component[b]			Redistribution component					
	1962–1965	1966–1969	1970–1972	1962–1965	1966–1969	1970–1972	1962–1965	1966–1969	1970–1972
$ 500– 1,000	97	98	95	97	98	96	1	3	1
1,001– 1,500	97	93	76	97	93	83	7	8	6
1,501– 2,000	89	84	78	88	85	79	6	9	5
2,001– 2,500	88	84	75	87	85	79	18	15	7
2,501– 3,000	89	82	79	89	83	82	13	10	9
3,001– 3,500	87	81	72	85	82	75	7	13	6
3,501– 4,000	87	80	71	87	82	75	12	9	10
4,001– 5,000	89	82	73	89	83	76	12	13	12
5,001– 6,000	90	79	66	90	80	71	5	12	6
6,001– 8,000	91	82	67	90	83	73	6	15	13
8,001–10,000	87	86	73	86	87	77	5	13	5
10,001–20,000	94	84	74	94	85	78	16	19	18
20,001+	88	64	75	88	67	79	4	1	3
Overall	90	83	75	90	84	79	112	140	101

[a]Annuity benefits employed to calculate the redistribution components were adjusted for earnings in excess of the 1972 earnings limit.

[b]Redistribution components were calculated by subtracting the mean annuity benefit level from the mean 1972 OAI benefit level reported as a percentage of the mean 1972 OAI benefit level. Raw data used to calculate the reported results are available upon request.

Table 5.11. Population Distribution for Married, Both-Retired Couples by Family Income in 1972 and Family Type

Family income in 1972	Two-earner[a]		One-earner[b]	
	Population size	Percentage distribution	Population size	Percentage distribution
$ 0- 2,000	3	0.5	29	4.0
2,001- 2,500	13	2.0	33	4.0
2,501- 3,000	13	2.0	46	6.0
3,001- 3,500	31	5.0	55	7.0
3,501- 4,000	46	7.5	72	9.0
4,001- 5,000	107	17.5	113	15.0
5,001- 6,000	91	15.0	98	13.0
6,001- 8,000	122	20.0	111	14.0
8,001-10,000	70	11.5	66	8.0
10,001-20,000	86	14.0	124	16.0
20,001+	32	5.0	33	4.0
Total	614	100.0	780	100.0

[a]Husband and wife are eligible for primary-worker benefits on their own accounts.

[b]Husband is eligible for primary-worker benefits on his own account, and the wife is not eligible for primary-worker benefits.

Generally speaking, entitled female workers received retirement benefits that were larger than dependent spouse benefits. One reason for the observed OAI benefit differential is that the nonworking woman's benefit is based on 50 percent of her husband's primary insurance amount (PIA), whereas the entitled female worker's benefit is based on her own PIA if it exceeds 50 percent of that of her spouse.

Working women received higher annuity benefits from an actuarially fair retirement system based on their actual contributions than nonworking women (column 2, table 5.13). Column 3 presents the difference between annuity benefits received by working and nonworking women based on actual contributions made by their husbands. The negative values in column 3 indicate that the working woman received a smaller annuity

Table 5.12. Effect of the Wife's Work Status on Wife-Only Benefit Incidence Holding Family Income Constant (Type-6, Indexed, Socioeconomic-Adjusted Survivorship Tables, and Earnings-Adjusted)

	Two-earner couple[a]					One-earner couple[b]				
	(1)	(2)	(3)	(4)		(5)	(6)	(7)	(8)	
Total family[c] income in 1972	Female OAI benefit level (mean)	Actu-arially fair benefit from wife's annuity	Actu-arially fair benefit from husband's annuity	Redistribu-tion component (a) 1-2-3	(b) $\frac{1-2-3}{1}$	Female OAI benefit level (mean)	Actu-arially fair benefit from wife's annuity	Actu-arially fair benefit from husband's annuity	Redistribu-tion component (a) 5-6-7	(b) $\frac{5-6-7}{5}$
$ 0- 2,000	506	29	26	451	89	418	0	35	383	92
2,001- 2,500	752	18	60	674	90	542	1	42	499	92
2,501- 3,000	1,023	38	70	915	89	702	1	89	612	87
3,001- 3,500	1,193	58	105	1,030	86	754	1	102	651	86
3,501- 4,000	1,210	62	140	1,008	83	912	1	143	768	84
4,001- 5,000	1,255	65	157	1,033	82	918	1	138	779	85
5,001- 6,000	1,316	61	182	1,073	82	929	1	172	756	81
6,001- 8,000	1,413	80	171	1,162	82	955	1	162	792	83
8,001-10,000	1,412	88	148	1,176	83	896	2	159	735	82
10,001-20,000	1,508	80	129	1,299	86	933	1	144	788	84
20,001+	1,596	87	159	1,350	85	942	2	134	806	86

[a]Husband and wife are eligible for primary-worker benefits on their own accounts.

[b]Husband is eligible for primary-worker benefits on his own account, and the wife is not eligible for primary-worker benefits.

[c]Total family income includes OAI benefits in 1972.

Table 5.13. Comparison of OAI and Type-6, Earnings-Adjusted Annuity Benefits for Married Women with Different Labor-Homemaker Choices Holding Family Income Constant

Total family[e] income in 1972	(1) Difference[c] between female OAI benefit levels	(2) Difference[b] between actuarially fair benefits from wife's annuity	(3) Difference[a] between actuarially fair benefits from husband's annuity	(4) Difference in[d] redistribution components as a percentage of OAI
$ 0- 2,000	88	29	-9	-3
2,001- 2,500	210	17	18	-2
2,501- 3,000	321	37	-19	+2
3,001- 3,500	439	57	3	0
3,501- 4,000	298	61	-3	-1
4,001- 5,000	337	64	19	-3
5,001- 6,000	387	60	10	+1
6,001- 8,000	458	79	9	-1
8,001-10,000	516	86	-11	+1
10,001-20,000	575	79	-15	+2
20,001+	654	85	25	-1

[a]Fifty percent of the two-earner woman's share of her husband's yearly annuity benefit less 50 percent of the one-earner woman's share of her husband's yearly annuity benefit.

[b]Fifty percent of the two-earner woman's yearly annuity benefit minus 50 percent of the one-earner woman's yearly annuity benefit.

[c]The mean level of OAI benefits received by a woman in a two-earner household less the mean level of benefits received by a woman in a one-earner household.

[d]The difference between redistribution components of women in two-earner and one-earner households.

[e]Total family income includes OAI benefits in 1972.

benefit from her husband's joint-and-two-thirds annuity than the non-working woman. On net, a working woman received higher annuity benefits based on the household's OAI contributions, and, because of her past contributions, she was afforded higher OAI benefits.

The difference in percentage of redistribution per dollar of OAI benefits for working and nonworking women is shown in column 4 of table 5.13. Working women received a higher percentage of redistribution in the following income categories: $2,501–3,000, $5,001–6,000, $8,001–10,000, and $10,001–20,000. But nonworking women received an equal or higher percentage of redistribution per dollar of OAI benefits in all other income categories. It appears that there was slightly more redistribution to nonworking women vis-à-vis working women. In absolute terms, however, working women paid in more dollars in the form of OAI contributions, and, in exchange, they received higher OAI benefit levels. The relatively narrow differential in redistribution components suggests that women, independent of work status, were treated almost equally in terms of redistribution.

The Effect of the Wife's Work Status on Husband-Only Benefit Incidence

The finding of roughly equal treatment among women with different labor-homemaker choices does not apply to men married to women who made different labor-homemaker choices. Tables 5.14 and 5.15 represent the male versions of tables 5.12 and 5.13. Note that the male redistribution components as a percentage of OAI benefits (columns 4b and 8b) are generally higher for males in one-earner households relative to their male counterparts in two-earner households. The percentage of redistribution measures follows the generally observed pattern—falling as family income rises. However, the variance in the pattern is slightly smaller for males in a one-earner household (97 to 92 percent). This implies that males in one-earner households with family incomes of $0–2,000 received 97 cents of redistribution for every dollar of OAI benefit. Similarly, males in the $5,001–10,000 income classes received 92 cents of redistribution per dollar of OAI benefit.

Generally, males in two-earner households received smaller OAI benefits (column 1, table 5.15), although males in two-earner families received higher combined annuity benefits based on the actual OAI contributions of both earners in the households. The difference in combined annuity benefits (columns 2 plus 3 in table 5.15) across household type is, in large part, a result of the annuity benefits received from the wife's joint-and-two-thirds annuity based on her actual OAI contributions. Column 4 in table 5.15 shows that males in one-earner households consistently received a larger percentage of redistribution from the OAI program than males in two-earner households.

The Effect of the Wife's Work Status on Family Benefit Incidence

Table 5.16 represents the benefit incidence across one-earner and two-earner households, holding constant family income in 1972. Column 7

Table 5.14. Effect of the Wife's Work Status on Husband-Only Benefit Incidence Holding Family Income Constant (Type-6, Indexed, Socioeconomic-Adjusted Survivorship Tables, and Earnings-Adjusted)

	Two-earner couple[a]					One-earner couple[b]				
	(1)	(2)	(3)	(4) Redistribution component		(5)	(6)	(7)	(8) Redistribution component	
Total family[c] income in 1972	Male OAI benefit level (mean)	Actuarially fair benefit from wife's annuity	Actuarially fair benefit from husband's annuity	(a) 1-2-3	(b) $\frac{1-2-3}{1}$	Male OAI benefit level (mean)	Actuarially fair benefit from wife's annuity	Actuarially fair benefit from husband's annuity	(a) 5-6-7	(b) $\frac{5-6-7}{5}$
$ 0- 2,000	906	29	26	851	94	1,026	0	35	991	97
2,001- 2,500	1,349	18	60	1,271	94	1,309	1	42	1,266	97
2,501- 3,000	1,521	38	70	1,413	93	1,604	1	89	1,514	94
3,001- 3,500	1,598	58	105	1,435	90	1,727	1	102	1,624	94
3,501- 4,000	1,961	62	140	1,759	90	1,995	1	143	1,851	93
4,001- 5,000	1,986	65	157	1,764	89	2,103	1	138	1,964	93
5,001- 6,000	2,150	61	182	1,907	89	2,092	1	172	1,919	92
6,001- 8,000	2,056	80	171	1,805	88	2,091	1	162	1,928	92
8,001-10,000	1,947	88	148	1,711	88	2,086	2	159	1,925	92
10,001-20,000	1,907	80	129	1,698	89	2,062	1	144	1,917	93
20,001+	2,197	87	159	1,951	89	2,110	2	134	1,974	94

[a]Husband and wife are eligible for primary-worker benefits on their own accounts.

[b]Husband is eligible for primary-worker benefits on his own account, and the wife is not eligible for primary-worker benefits.

[c]Total family income includes OAI benefits in 1972.

Table 5.15. Comparison of OAI and Type-6, Adjusted Annuity Benefits for Married Men in One-Earner and Two-Earner Households Holding Family Income Constant

Total family[e] income in 1972	(1) Difference[c] between male OAI benefit levels	(2) Difference[b] between actuarially fair benefits from wife's annuity	(3) Difference[a] between actuarially fair benefits from husband's annuity	(4) Difference in[d] redistribution components as a percentage of OAI
$ 0- 2,000	-120	29	-9	-3
2,001- 2,500	40	17	18	-3
2,501- 3,000	-83	37	-19	-1
3,001- 3,500	-129	57	3	-4
3,501- 4,000	-34	61	-3	-3
4,001- 5,000	-117	64	19	-4
5,001- 6,000	58	60	10	-3
6,001- 8,000	-35	79	9	-4
8,001-10,000	-139	86	-11	-4
10,001-20,000	-155	79	-15	-4
20,001+	87	85	25	-5

[a]Fifty percent of the two-earner man's yearly annuity benefit minus 50 percent of the one-earner man's yearly annuity benefit.

[b]Fifty percent of the two-earner man's share of his wife's yearly annuity benefit less 50 percent of the one-earner man's share of his wife's yearly annuity benefit.

[c]The mean level of OAI benefits received by a man in a two-earner household less the mean level of benefits received by a man in a one-earner household.

[d]The difference between redistribution components of men in two-earner and one-earner households.

[e]Total family income includes OAI benefits in 1972.

indicates that, except for the lowest income category, family OAI benefit levels were higher for two-earner households vis-à-vis one-earner households. In addition, two-earner households received higher family benefits from an actuarially fair retirement system (column 8). All family units, independent of household types, received positive income transfers from the OAI program (columns 3 and 6). Moreover, the one-earner household received a larger percentage of redistribution relative to the two-earner household for all income categories (column 9).

The Importance of the Household Type in Explaining the Benefit Incidence

The tabular results regarding the percentage of redistribution by sex and household type across family income classes (columns 4b and 8b, tables 5.12 and 5.14) are summarized in figure 5.3. Note that the percentage of redistribution received by women, independent of work status, is generally lower than the comparable measure for men. The observed male-to-female differential in redistribution is consistent across all income categories. But, looking at the redistribution curves for women by household types in figure 5.3, it appears that the sizes and patterns of the redistribution measure for women in one-earner and two-earner households are very similar. The observed similarity suggests that, although women with different work statuses paid in different amounts of OAI contributions, they were treated equally in terms of the percentage of OAI benefits representing redistribution from the current working generation.

The redistribution patterns for males in one-earner and two-earner households are similar; however, the absolute size of the redistribution measure varies significantly by household type. It is clear from figure 5.3 that the percentage of redistribution for males in one-earner households is substantially larger than the comparable measure for males in two-earner households across *all* income categories. One reason for this obvious size disparity is the very small (or zero) annuity benefit received from the nonworking wife's joint-and-two-thirds annuity. Because his wife's yearly annuity payment is generally equal to zero, the male's redistribution component is larger.

Although males in one-earner households received preferential treatment from the OAI program vis-à-vis males in two-earner households and females, working women as a group received a significantly smaller percentage of redistribution when compared to working males. There are several reasons for the smaller redistribution components received by working women. First, entitled women frequently claim reduced benefits. In 1967, 67 percent of the married female retired workers aged 65 and older received reduced benefits. By 1971, the proportion had increased to 76 percent. The proportion of beneficiary women with reduced benefits puts downward pressure on mean OAI benefit levels used to calculate the redistribution components.

Second, working women have smaller primary insurance amounts relative to working men because of their lower earnings and intermittent

Table 5.16. Effect of the Wife's Work Status on Family Benefit Incidence Holding Total Family Income Constant

Total family income in 1972	Two-earner couple			One-earner couple			Comparison		
	(1) Family OAI benefit level[a]	(2) Family annuity benefit[b]	(3) Redistribution component as a percentage of family OAI benefits (1)	(4) Family OAI benefit level[a]	(5) Family annuity benefit[b]	(6) Redistribution component as a percentage of family OAI benefits (4)	(7) Difference in family OAI benefits (1)-(4)	(8) Difference in family annuity benefit (2)-(5)	(9) Difference in redistribution components (3)-(6)
$ 0- 2,000	1,411	111	92	1,433	71	95	-22	40	-3
2,001- 2,500	2,101	156	93	1,851	87	95	250	69	-2
2,501- 3,000	2,544	217	91	2,306	181	92	238	36	-1
3,001- 3,500	2,791	328	88	2,481	208	92	310	120	-4
3,501- 4,000	3,171	404	87	2,907	289	90	264	115	-3
4,001- 5,000	3,242	443	86	3,021	279	91	221	164	-5
5,001- 6,000	3,466	487	86	3,021	346	89	445	141	-3
6,001- 8,000	3,470	502	86	3,046	326	89	424	176	-3
8,001-10,000	3,359	472	86	2,983	322	89	376	150	-3
10,001-20,000	3,414	417	88	2,995	289	90	419	128	-2
20,001+	3,793	493	87	3,051	271	91	742	222	-4

[a]Combined OAI benefit received by the husband and wife in 1972.

[b]Combined annuity benefit received by the husband and wife.

Figure 5.3. Graphical Comparison of Redistribution Components, Expressed in Percentage Terms, by Sex and Household Type

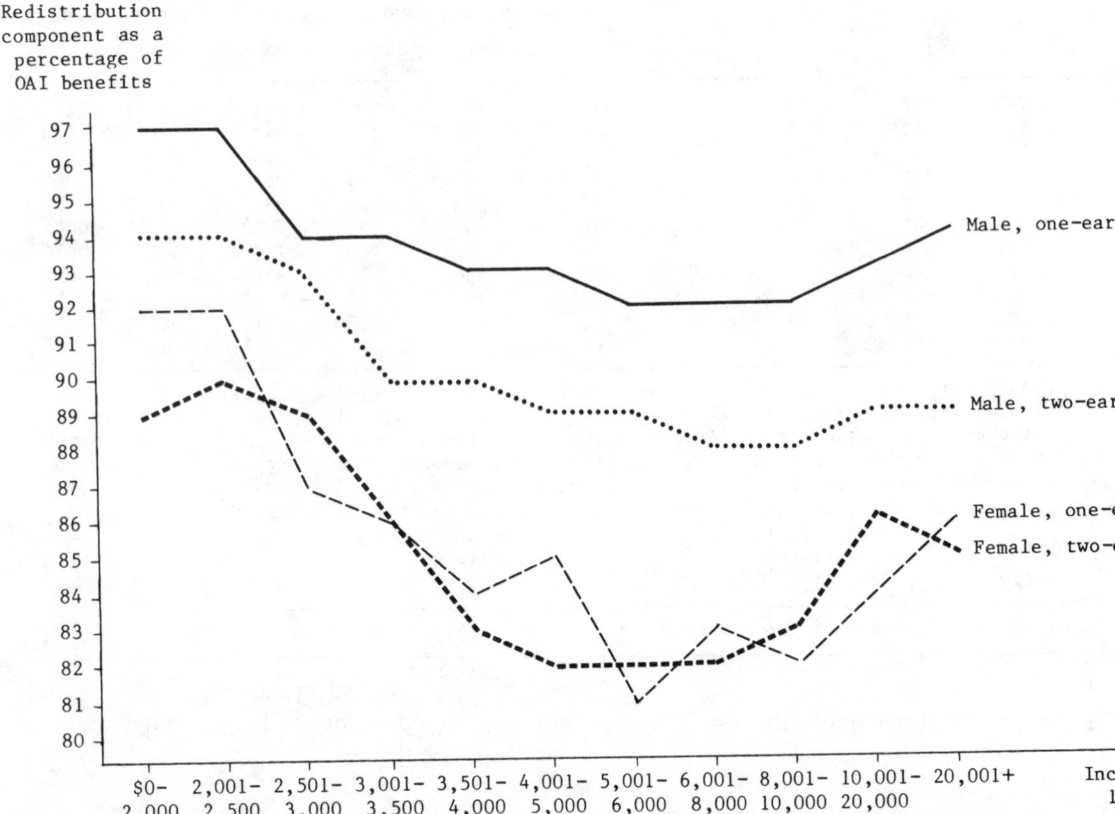

labor force participation. In 1971, a significant proportion of retired female workers, especially the dually entitled, were entitled to the minimum PIA. Half of the dually entitled female workers, in 1971, were entitled to the minimum PIA compared to 7 percent of male workers. Differences in PIA distributions for male and female workers reflect differences in work histories. Men generally work for longer periods of time at higher earnings, resulting in higher PIAs.

The last reason concerns the annuity benefit received by working women from their husband's past OAI contributions. Since the male worker pays into the system longer and, in addition, receives higher earnings, he has a larger accumulated tax contribution to purchase a joint-and-two-thirds annuity at retirement. Assuming community property ownership of the actuarially fair benefit, the wife receives half of her husband's yearly annuity benefit (in an actuarially fair system) purchased with his OAI contributions at retirement. The wife's redistribution component is determined by subtracting her OAI benefit level from her share of the yearly family annuity benefit based on her OAI contribution and her husband's OAI contributions.

Figure 5.4 summarizes the tabular results in columns 3 and 6 in table 5.16. The distribution of redistribution components by household type illustrated in figure 5.4 shows that one-earner families, on average, received preferential treatment from the OAI program. Again, the preferential status of one-earner families is explained by the nominal contributions made by the nonworking spouse in the one-earner family.

The Progressivity of the OAI Program by Household Type

The end-point approach to determining progressivity suggests that the program is weakly progressive: the variances for women and men in two-earner families are 90–82 and 94–88, respectively, and the variances for women and men in one-earner families are 92–81 and 97–92, respectively. Progressivity assessment based on the patterned approach shows the program to be selectively progressive given the generally observed inverse relationship between the percentage of redistribution and total family income. However, the high-income-group-comparison approach exposes strong regressive features for women in both household types, mild regressive features for men in one-earner households, and strong progressive features for men in two-earner households.

Figure 5.5 applies to females only and shows the program to be progressive at income levels less than $3,500 but strongly regressive at income levels greater than $3,500. Middle-income females, especially, are made worse off relative to the highest income group of females, independent of

Figure 5.4. Distribution of Redistribution Components, Expressed in Percentage Terms, by Household Type

Figure 5.5. Progressivity of the OAI Program by Household Type: Females Only

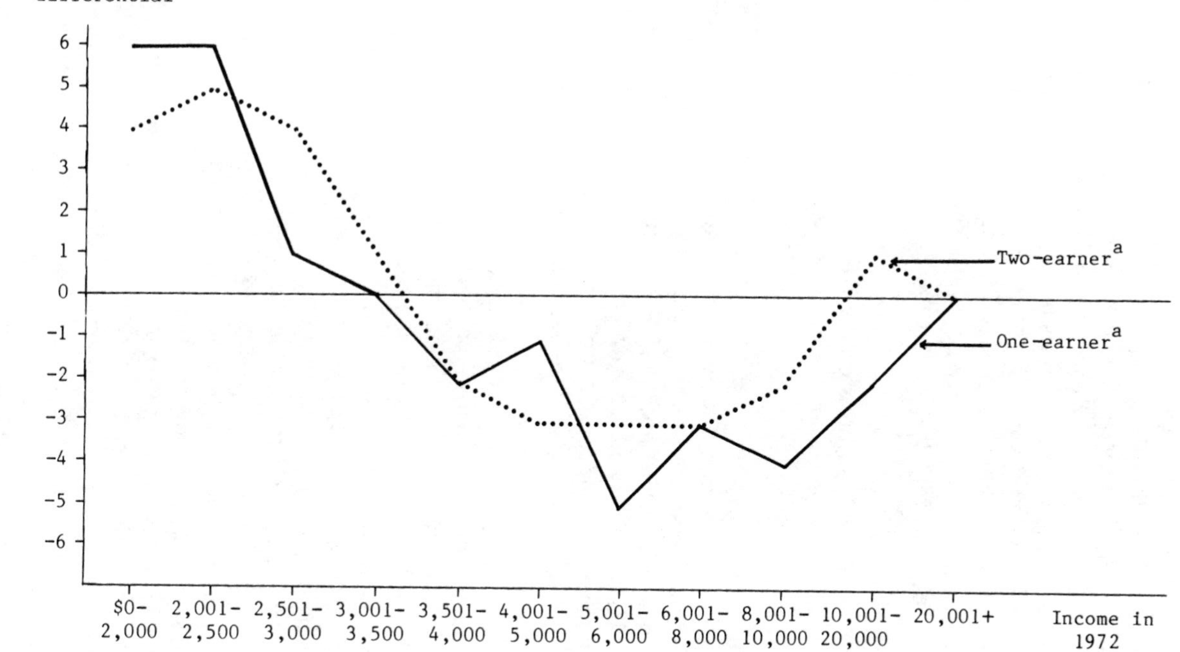

[a]Percentage of redistribution for a family income level minus percentage of redistribution for richest income level.

household type. The program does not appear to be as regressive when focusing on males only (figure 5.6). The program demonstrated classic progressive features for males in two-earner households for income levels of $5,000 or less, and it demonstrated only slight regressive features for the $6,000–20,000 range. The program has a narrow progressive area (0–3,000) for males in one-earner households and somewhat classic regressive features for income levels in excess of $3,000. Figure 5.7 is based on the household unit sorted by household type. Again, the program had classic progressive features at low income levels ($0–3,500) but had regressive features at higher income levels. The program is more progressive and less regressive for two-earner relative to one-earner households.[4]

The Effect of Marital Status on the Distribution of Income: Single and Married, Both-Retired Households

Redistribution components expressed in percentage terms are presented for single, one-earner, and two-earner households by sex in figure 5.8. Women, independent of marital status, have redistribution curves that are very similar in pattern and level, excluding the $2,001–2,500 income category. The relatively narrow difference in redistribution measures indicates that women, independent of work and marital status, receive roughly equal treatment in terms of the percentage of redistribution per dollar of OAI benefits.

The finding of roughly equal treatment among women with different labor-homemaker and marital choices does not apply to similar comparisons among single men and men married to women who made different labor-homemaker choices. Since the differences between one-earner and two-earner married men were discussed in the last section, they will not be discussed again. Instead, the more dramatic differences between single and married men will be examined.

Single men have a more erratic redistribution curve than their married counterparts. Also, the absolute level of redistribution is significantly lower for single men than married men. Specifically, single men received redistribution components that were 7 to 15 or 11 to 19 percentage points smaller than the comparable measure for married men in two-earner households and married men in one-earner households, respectively. Single men receive lower returns on their OAI contributions vis-à-vis married men because of the difference in their insurance coverage. A married man purchases double annuity coverage, insurance covering himself and his wife, with his compounded OAI contributions. A single man purchases individual annuity coverage only. Other things equal, since the married

Figure 5.6 Progressivity of the OAI Program by Household Type: Males Only

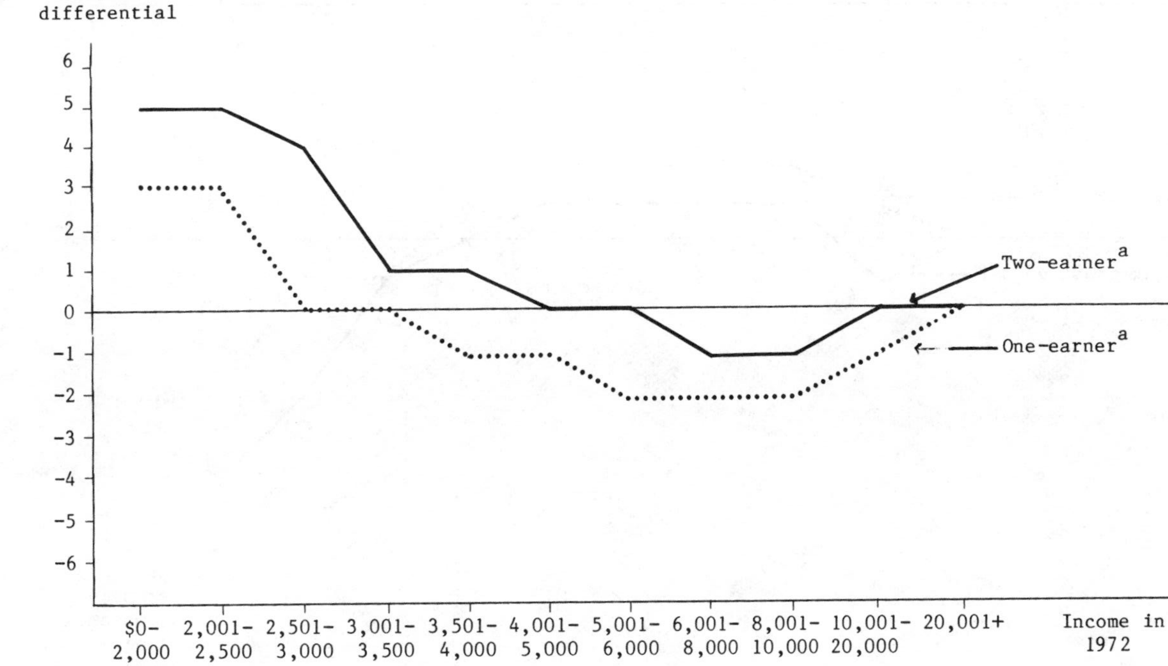

[a]Percentage of redistribution for a family income level minus percentage of redistribution for richest income level.

Figure 5.7 Progressivity of the OAI Program by Household Type

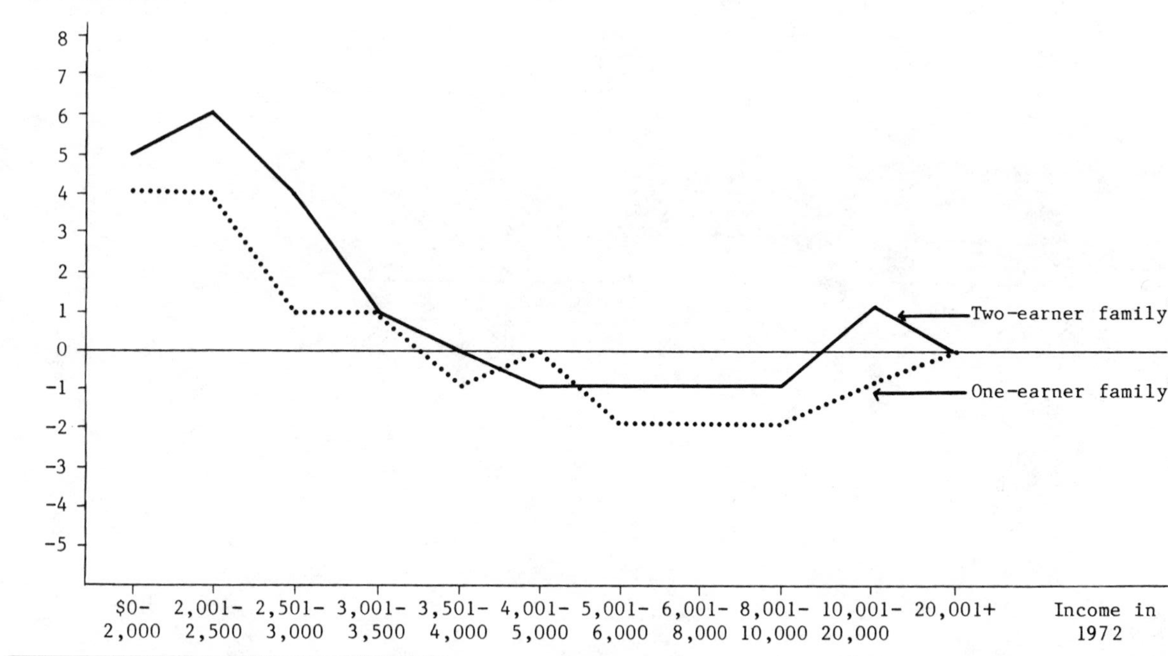

[a]Percentage of redistribution for a family income level minus percentage of redistribution for richest income level.

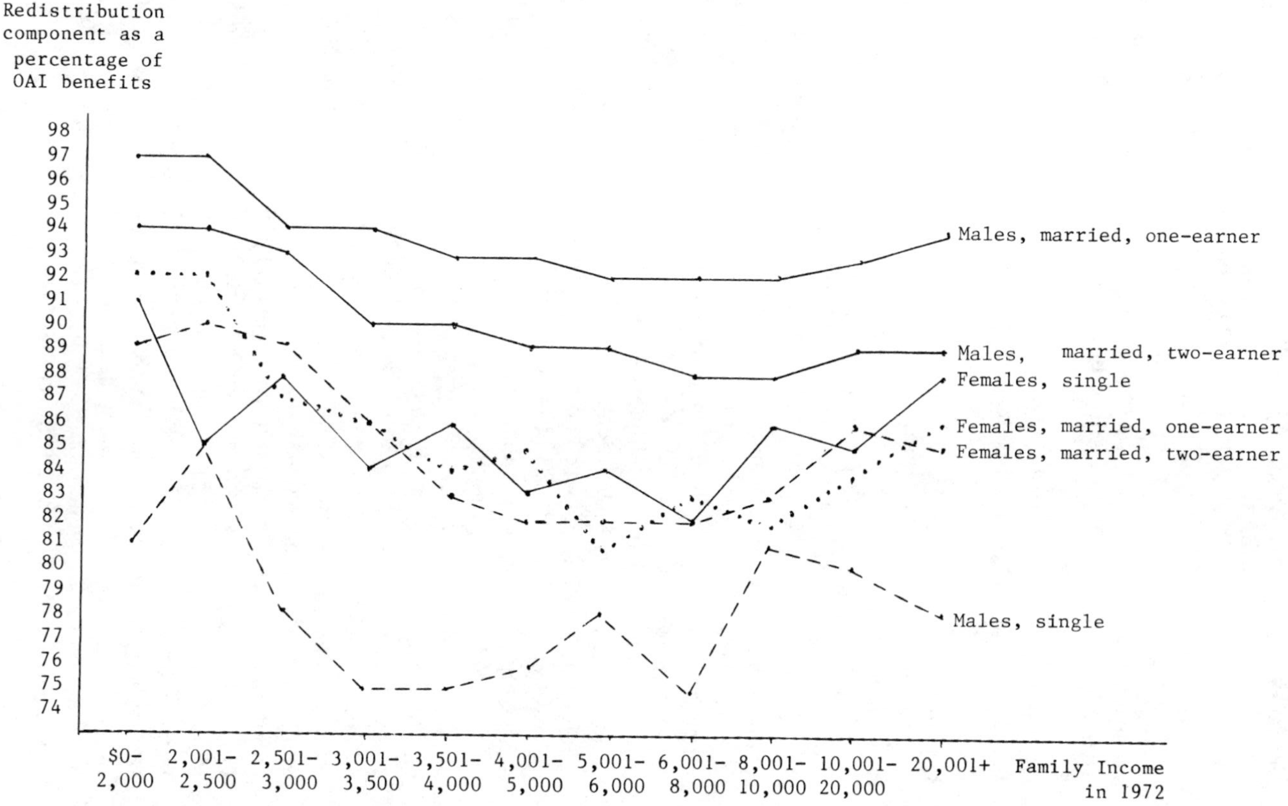

Figure 5.8 Graphical Comparison of Redistribution Components, Expressed in Percentage Terms, by Sex and Household Type

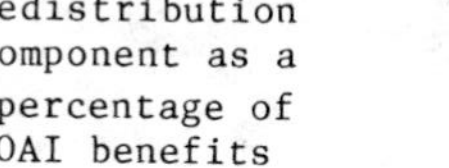

man purchases double coverage, his annuity payment is smaller and, subsequently, his redistribution component is larger.

Single men fare less well under OAI than other groups because 1) they are forced to participate in a retirement program premised on a married family model, and 2) they have less favorable survivorship rates. Single women fare better than their male counterparts because of their greater longevity, which tends to reduce the size of their annuity benefit.

The Effect of Social Security Payments on the Distribution of Income: Both-Retired Households Only

The effect of Social Security benefits on the distribution of income among elderly households was examined by dividing into quintile groups all married couples in which both members were collecting OAI benefits between 1962 and 1972. Table 5.17 presents the distribution of income before and after payment of Social Security benefits. The distribution of personal income, exclusive of benefits, was highly skewed; the poorest 60 percent of the elderly population had less than 20 percent of personal income, whereas the richest 20 percent of the elderly population held 60 percent of personal income. The addition of the husband's OAI benefits did reduce the skewness in the distribution of income. Column 2 displays the distribution of personal income inclusive of the husband's OAI benefits but exclusive of the wife's OAI benefits. In this case, the poorest 60 percent received 30 percent of personal income, whereas the richest 20 percent received just under 50 percent of personal income.

Column 3 displays the distribution of personal income after all family OAI benefits were apportioned. The distribution of personal income was, in spite of the Social Security program, skewed in favor of the richest quintile, but the program did increase the relative share of personal income received by the poorest 60 percent of the elderly. After receipt of all family OAI benefits, the poorest 60 percent had 34 percent of personal income, whereas the richest quintile received 45 percent of personal income. Also, the husband's share of OAI benefits had the greatest redistributional impact. This is expected, since the absolute size of the male's OAI benefit generally exceeded that of the female because of the male's higher average earnings and stronger labor force attachment and because females typically collect auxiliary (dependents) benefits.

Table 5.18 looks at the distribution of Social Security benefits by percentage share. Married couples in the sample received approximately $4.2 million in OAI benefits in 1972, 65 percent of which was paid to male beneficiaries and 35 percent to female beneficiaries.

Overall, Social Security benefits were proportionally distributed to

Table 5.17. Distribution of Income for Both-Retired Population Before and After Payment of Social Security Benefits

	(1) Distribution of personal income before social security	(2) Distribution of personal income after husband's OAI benefits	(3) Distribution of personal income after family OAI benefits	Mean personal income		
				Without social security	With husband benefit only	With family OAI benefits
Poorest quintile	1.0%	6.0%	8.0%	$210	$2,142	$3,141
Second quintile	6.0	10.0	11.0	1,305	3,255	4,331
Third quintile	11.0	14.0	15.0	2,535	4,557	5,635
Fourth quintile	21.0	21.0	21.0	4,913	6,877	7,973
Richest quintile	61.0	49.0	45.0	14,337	16,270	17,400
Total	100.0	100.0	100.0			

Table 5.18. Distribution of Social Security Benefits to Both-Retired Population by Percentage Share

Quintile group	All OAI benefits	Male beneficiaries' OAI benefits	Female beneficiaries' OAI benefits	Percentage gain in personal income		
				Household	Male beneficiary	Female beneficiary
Total	4,231,935	2,732,532	1,499,403			
Percentage	100.0	64.50	35.43			
Poorest quintile	19.3%	19.7%	18.6%	1,394%	919%	475%
Second quintile	19.9	19.9	20.0	232	149	83
Third quintile	20.4	20.6	20.1	122	80	42
Fourth quintile	20.2	20.1	20.3	62	40	22
Richest quintile	20.1	19.7	21.0	21	13	8
Total	100.0	100.0	100.0			

households, male beneficiaries, and female beneficiaries. Nevertheless, the roughly proportional distribution of OAI benefits significantly improved the level of personal income for the poorest 60 percent of the elderly population. The poorest quintile received 19.3 percent of all Social Security benefits paid to both-retired, married couples in 1972, which increased its level of personal income by 1,394 percent.

In conclusion, column 1 of table 5.17 indicates that the distribution of personal income before Social Security was sharply skewed in favor of the richest income quintile. The single-period analysis of OAI transfers shows that, although the distribution of personal income after the addition of Social Security benefits was not distributed particularly evenly, there was a significant change toward increasing income equality as a result of the program's intergenerational transfer mechanism and income-smoothing feature.[5] A closer look at the disbursement of OAI benefits (table 5.18) shows that benefits were, at best, proportionally distributed across quintile groups, but the largest relative gains in the level of personal income, before and after Social Security benefits, were realized by the poorest 60 percent of the elderly population.

The use of single-period analysis to assess the distributional impact of Social Security is insightful, but it can be very misleading, since it fails to distinguish between the intergenerational transfer and income-smoothing features of the program. Because benefits are contingent on past OAI contributions, they are a mixture of the return on past contributions, redistribution within a retirement cohort, and redistribution across generations. The following tables in this section focus on the distributional impact of the intergenerational transfer mechanism only; that is, the income-smoothing feature has been stripped away by use of type-6 annuity counterfactuals. Table 5.19 presents the distribution of redistribution components by quintile group, controlling for family type and sex. The distribution of income before and after apportioning the redistribution component is displayed in table 5.20.

Similar to the distribution pattern of Social Security benefits, the redistribution components were distributed roughly equally across quintile groups, independent of family type and sex (table 5.19). Note that the poorest quintile of one-earner households received approximately 21 percent of all intergenerational transfers to males and females in one-earner households. Column 4 in table 5.19 indicates that spousal benefits were, at best, proportionally distributed to dependent spouses of male workers and, therefore, were not distributed principally to needy dependent spouses as intended by the spousal benefit provision (consistent with Holden [1979 and 1982]).

Table 5.20 displays the distribution of income for married, both-

Table 5.19. Distribution of Redistribution Components by Quintile Group Controlling for Family Type and Sex

	Two-earner			One-earner		
	(1) Female's share of redistribution[a]	(2) Male's share of redistribution[a]	(3) Household's share of redistribution[a]	(4) Female's share of redistribution[a]	(5) Male's share of redistribution[a]	(6) Household's share of redistribution[a]
Poorest quintile	16.7%	18.1%	17.5%	20.8%	21.1%	21.0%
Second quintile	20.1	20.5	20.4	19.7	19.4	19.4
Third quintile	20.3	22.0	21.3	18.9	19.4	19.3
Fourth quintile	21.0	20.4	20.6	19.6	19.6	19.6
Richest quintile	21.9	18.9	20.1	21.0	20.5	20.6
Total	674,798	1,075,773	1,767,702	560,920	1,416,564	1,989,561

[a] Redistribution component calculations are based on type-6, earnings-adjusted counterfactuals.

Table 5.20. Distribution of Income for Married, Both-Retired Population Before and After Apportioning the Redistribution Component

Quintile group	All households		Two-earner household			One-earner household		
	(1) Distribution of personal income before social security	(2) Distribution of personal income after RC[a]	(3) Distribution of personal income before RC[a]	(4) Distribution of personal income after RC[a]	(5) Net effect	(6) Distribution of personal income before RC[a]	(7) Distribution of personal income after RC[a]	(8) Net effect
Poorest quintile	1.0%	7.7%	0.7%	7.1%	+6.4	1.1%	8.2%	+7.1
Second quintile	6.0	10.9	5.6	11.2	+5.6	5.6	10.6	+5.0
Third quintile	11.0	14.3	11.6	15.2	+3.6	10.4	13.5	+3.1
Fourth quintile	21.0	20.7	21.1	20.9	−0.2	21.1	20.6	−0.5
Richest quintile	61.0	46.4	60.0	45.6	−14.4	61.8	47.1	−14.7

[a]Redistribution component calculations are based on type-6, earnings-adjusted counterfactuals.

retired populations before and after apportioning the redistribution components. Comparing column 2 of table 5.20 and column 3 of table 5.17, it is clear that single-period analysis tends to slightly overstate the distributional impact of the OAI program. The intergenerational transfer mechanism did increase income equality but not to the extent that single-period analysis indicates or the social adequacy objective would seem to dictate.

6

A Formal Specification of the Regression Model

This chapter presents the single and married regression models estimated to isolate the effect of worker characteristics on the percentage of redistribution. The first section includes a description of the generalized quadratic models for single and married households and the model variables. Model variables, independent and dependent, are discussed in detail in the next section.

Functional Form

Single Model

The following generalized quadratic model was estimated to isolate the partial effect of worker-specific characteristics on the percentage of redistribution X:[1]

$$\begin{aligned}X = {} & \beta_0 + \beta_1\text{LTEAR} + \beta_2\text{LTEAR2} + \beta_3\text{SEX} + \beta_4\text{RACE} + \\ & \beta_5\text{SERLEN} + \beta_6\text{SERLEN2} + \beta_7\text{RAGER1} + \\ & \beta_8\text{RAGER2} + \beta_9\text{RAGER3} + \beta_{10}\text{RCOHORT1} + \\ & \beta_{11}\text{RCOHORT2} + \beta_{12}\text{EDU1} + \beta_{13}\text{EDU2} + \beta_{14}\text{EDU3} + \\ & \beta_{15}\text{EDU4} \end{aligned} \tag{6.1}$$

where the dependent and independent variables are defined in tables 6.1 and 6.2, respectively, and explained in the next section. Four permutations of the generalized single model were estimated; the models differed by specification of the dependent variable only.

The reasons for constructing these four different models were: first, to see if variables significant in explaining the percentage of redistribution changed under various counterfactual definitions; and second, to determine if there were any unexpected sign reversals in the parameter estimates. Since this study attempts to account for the effect of worker characteristics and program features on the size of the redistribution com-

Table 6.1. Definitions of the Dependent Variables Used in the Single Regression Equations

Variable	Description
RRC_{ij}	The nonindexed, nonearnings-adjusted redistribution component for individual j as a percentage of individual j's 1972 OAI benefit level where i equals type-1, type-2, or type-3 annuity counterfactual
RRC^*_{ij}	The indexed, nonearnings-adjusted redistribution component for individual j as a percentage of individual j's 1972 OAI benefit level where i equals type-4, type-5, or type-6 annuity counterfactual
$ERRC_{ij}$	The nonindexed, earnings-adjusted redistribution component for individual j as a percentage of individual j's 1972 OAI benefit level where i equals type-1, type-2, or type-3 annuity counterfactual adjusted by the earnings test
$ERRC^*_{ij}$	The indexed, earnings-adjusted redistribution component for individual j as a percentage of individual j's 1972 OAI benefit level where i equals type-4, type-5, or type-6 annuity counterfactual adjusted by the earnings test

ponent, 12 measures of redistribution were used as dependent variables. Each measure was calculated identically, in a technical sense, but different annuity counterfactuals were employed in each measure to net out the worker-purchased insurance component. For future reference, the estimation of model 6.1 with dependent variables RRC_{ij}, RRC^*_{ij}, $ERRC_{ij}$ and $ERRC^*_{ij}$ will be referred to as models 1, 2, 3, and 4, respectively. Each model is estimated using three different mortality rate assumptions.

Married Model

To isolate the partial effect of family-specific characteristics on the percentage of redistribution for a husband-and-wife family unit Y, the following generalized quadratic model was estimated:[2, 3]

$$\begin{aligned}Y = {} & \beta_0 + \beta_1 FLTEAR + \beta_2 FLTEAR2 + \beta_3 RACE + \beta_4 SERLEN + \\ & \beta_{5-}SERLEN + \beta_6 SERLEN2 + \beta_{7-}SERLEN2 + \\ & \beta_8 RAGER1 + \beta_9 RAGER2 + \beta_{10} RAGER3 + \\ & \beta_{11-}RAGER1 + \beta_{12-}RAGER2 + \beta_{13} RCOHORT1 + \\ & \beta_{14} RCOHORT2 + \beta_{15-}RCOHORT1 + \beta_{16-}RCOHORT2 + \\ & \beta_{17} EDU1 + \beta_{18} EDU2 + \beta_{19} EDU3 + \beta_{20} EDU4 + \\ & \beta_{21-}EDU1 + \beta_{22-}EDU2 + \beta_{23-}EDU3 + \beta_{24-}EDU4 \qquad (6.2)\end{aligned}$$

Table 6.2. Definitions of the Independent Variables Used in Single Regression Equations

Variable	Description
LTEAR	Accumulated value of lifetime earnings (in hundreds of thousands)
LTEAR2	LTEAR squared
SEX	Dummy variable for sex: 0 for male, 1 for female
RACE	Dummy variable for race: 0 for white, 1 for nonwhite
SERLEN	Service length in covered employment
SERLEN2	SERLEN squared
RAGER1	Dummy variable for retirement age: 1 for age 62-64, 0 otherwise
RAGER2	Dummy variable for retirement age: 1 for age 66-71, 0 otherwise
RAGER3	Dummy variable for retirement age: 1 for age 72 and older, 0 otherwise
RCOHORT1	Dummy variable for retirement cohort: 1 for year 1962-1965, 0 otherwise
RCOHORT2	Dummy variable for retirement cohort: 1 for year 1966-1968, 0 otherwise
EDU1	Dummy variable for years of education completed: 1 for years 0-7, 0 otherwise
EDU2	Dummy variable for years of education completed: 1 for years 9-11, 0 otherwise
EDU3	Dummy variable for years of education completed: 1 for year 12, 0 otherwise
EDU4	Dummy variable for years of education completed: 1 for years 13 or more, 0 otherwise

where the dependent and independent variables are defined in tables 6.3 and 6.4, respectively,.and explained in the next section.

Again, 12 versions of model 6.2 were estimated, differing by dependent variable only. The dependent variables are labeled FAM_{ij}, FAM^*_{ij}, $EFAM_{ij}$, and $EFAM^*_{ij}$. The estimation of model 6.2 using FAM_{ij}, FAM^*_{ij}, $EFAM_{ij}$, and $EFAM^*_{ij}$ will be subsequently referred to as models 5, 6, 7, and 8, respectively. Each model is estimated using three different mortality rate assumptions.

Regression Variables

Dependent Variables

Twelve annuity counterfactuals were constructed for each household type, differing by program feature or life contingency assumption. Annuity counterfactuals distinguish one dependent variable from another. Recall that annuity counterfactuals were constructed to disentangle the entitled insurance payment of the OAI benefit from the redistribution payment. Counterfactuals range from traditional life annuities based on highly aggregated survivorship assumptions to indexed, earnings-adjusted life annuities reflecting highly disaggregated survivorship assumptions. The single and married generalized models are estimated using slightly different dependent variables to isolate how specific survivorship assumptions or program features influence the redistributional incidence of the OAI program. The following subsections will describe how each dependent variable was calculated for each household type.

Table 6.3. Definitions of the Dependent Variables Used in the Married Regression Equations

Variable	Description
FAM_{ij}	The nonindexed, nonearnings-adjusted redistribution component for family j as a percentage of family j's 1972 OAI benefit level where i equals type-1, type-2, or type-3 annuity counterfactual
FAM^{*}_{ij}	The indexed, nonearnings-adjusted redistribution component for family j as a percentage of family j's 1972 OAI benefit level where i equals type-4, type-5, or type-6 annuity counterfactual
$EFAM_{ij}$	The nonindexed, earnings-adjusted redistribution component for family j as a percentage of family j's 1972 OAI benefit level where i equals type-1, type-2, or type-3 annuity counterfactual adjusted by the earnings test
$EFAM^{*}_{ij}$	The indexed, earnings-adjusted redistribution component for family j as a percentage of family j's 1972 OAI benefit level where i equals type-4, type-5, or type-6 annuity counterfactual adjusted by the earnings test

Table 6.4. Definitions of the Independent Variables Used in Married Regression Equations

Variables	Description
FLTEAR	Accumulated value of family lifetime earnings (in hundreds of thousands)
FLTEAR2	FLTEAR squared
RACE	Dummy variable for race: 0 for white, 1 for nonwhite
SERLEN (_SERLEN)	Service length in covered employment for wife (husband)
SERLEN2 (_SERLEN2)	SERLEN (_SERLEN) squared
RAGER1 (_RAGER1)	Dummy variable for wife's (husband's) retirement age: 1 for age 62-64, 0 otherwise
RAGER2 (_RAGER2)	Dummy variable for wife's (husband's) retirement age: 1 for age 66-71, 0 otherwise
RAGER3	Dummy variable for wife's retirement age: 1 for age 72 and older, 0 otherwise
RCOHORT1 (_RCOHORT1)	Dummy variable for wife's (husband's) retirement cohort: 1 for year 1962-1965, 0 otherwise
RCOHORT2 (_RCOHORT2)	Dummy variable for wife's (husband's) retirement cohort: 1 for year 1966-1968, 0 otherwise
EDU1 (_EDU1)	Dummy variable for years of education completed by wife (husband): 1 for years 0-7, 0 otherwise
EDU2 (_EDU2)	Dummy variable for years of education completed by wife (husband): 1 for years 9-11, 0 otherwise
EDU3 (_EDU3)	Dummy variable for years of education completed by wife (husband): 1 for year 12, 0 otherwise
EDU4 (_EDU4)	Dummy variable for years of education completed by wife (husband): 1 for years 13 or more, 0 otherwise

Percentage of redistribution for the single model. There are four generic measures of redistribution for each single household. Each generic measure is distinguished by a program feature (with or without indexing; with or without earnings adjustments), and, within each measure, three survivorship probability assumptions were imposed (gender-merged, sex-race-distinct, socioeconomic-adjusted). The calculations used to determine the percentage of a redistribution under various assumptions for single households are as follows:

$$RRC_{ij} = \frac{BEN72_j - TB_{ij}}{BEN72_j} \times 100 \tag{6.3}$$

for i = type-1, type-2, type-3,

$$RRC^*_{ij} = \frac{BEN72_j - TB^*_{ij}}{BEN72_j} \times 100 \tag{6.4}$$

for i = type-4, type-5, type-6,

$$ERRC_{ij} = \frac{BEN72_j - ATB_{ij}}{BEN72_j} \times 100 \tag{6.5}$$

for i = type-1, type-2, type-3,

$$ERRC^*_{ij} = \frac{BEN72_j - ATB^*_{ij}}{BEN72_j} \times 100 \tag{6.6}$$

for i = type-4, type-5, type-6,

where BEN72 = 1972 OAI benefit amounts; TB_{ij} = nonindexed, nonearnings-adjusted type-i annuity benefit for individual j; TB^*_{ij} = indexed, non-earnings-adjusted type-i annuity benefit for individual j; ATB_{ij} = nonindexed, earnings-adjusted type-i annuity benefit for individual j; and ATB^*_{ij} = indexed, earnings-adjusted type-i annuity benefit for individual j.

Percentage of redistribution for the married model. The four generic measures of redistribution for each married household are:

$$FAM_{ij} = \frac{FBEN72_j - TB_{ij} - {}_{-}TB_{ij}}{FBEN72_j} \tag{6.7}$$

for i = type-1, type-2, type-3,

$$FAM^*_{ij} = \frac{FBEN72_j - TB^*_{ij} - {}_{-}TB^*_{ij}}{FBEN72_j} \tag{6.8}$$

for i = type-4, type-5, type-6,

$$EFAM_{ij} = \frac{FBEN72_j - ATB_{ij} - {}_{-}ATB_{ij}}{FBEN72_j} \tag{6.9}$$

for i = type-1, type-2, type-3,

$$\mathrm{EFAM}^*_{ij} = \frac{\mathrm{FBEN72}_j - \mathrm{ATB}^*_{ij} - {}_{-}\mathrm{ATB}^*_{ij}}{\mathrm{FBEN72}_j} \tag{6.10}$$

for i = type-4, type-5, type-6,

where FBEN72 = the sum of the wife and husband's 1972 OAI benefit amounts; TB_{ij} ($_{-}TB_{ij}$) = nonindexed, nonearnings-adjusted type-i annuity benefit for the wife (husband) in household j; TB^*_{ij} ($_{-}TB^*_{ij}$) = indexed, nonearnings-adjusted type-i annuity benefit for the wife (husband) in household j; ATB_{ij} ($_{-}ATB_{ij}$) = nonindexed, earnings-adjusted type-i annuity benefit for the wife (husband) in household j; and ATB^*_{ij} ($_{-}ATB^*_{ij}$) = indexed, earnings-adjusted type-i annuity benefit for the wife (husband) in household j.

Independent Variables

Accumulated value of lifetime earnings. The lifetime earnings variables (LTEAR, LTEAR2; FLTEAR, FLTEAR2) are two of four quantitative variables included in the generalized polynominal model. LTEAR reflects the individual's lifetime earnings stream on the date of retirement by a single number. FLTEAR is the sum of the husband and wife's lifetime earnings streams. LTEAR and FLTEAR were expected to have negative coefficients, whereas LTEAR2 and FLTEAR2 were expected to have positive coefficients. The summary measure of lifetime earnings was calculated assuming: 1) annual reported taxable earnings (REP_i) were received at the beginning of each year, and 2) the earnings stream was truncated on the date of retirement (YBEGIN2). Accordingly, the present value of the worker's lifetime real taxable earnings on the date of retirement is:

$$\mathrm{LTEAR} = \sum_{i=\mathrm{EYEAR}}^{\mathrm{YBEGIN2}} \frac{\mathrm{REP}_i}{C_i} \left[\prod_{j=i}^{\mathrm{YBEGIN2}} (1 + r_j) \right] \tag{6.11}$$

where YBEGIN2 = a year of retirement; EYEAR = year of entry into covered employment; REP_i = annual reported earnings in year i; C_i = consumer price index in year i; and r_j = annual real interest rate in year j. The percentage distribution of LTEAR for single households only appears in table 6.5. Table 6.6 displays the percentage distribution of FLTEAR for married households.

The summary measure of lifetime earnings differs from the simple sum of annual reported earnings by the weighting of annual reported earnings by the annual real interest rate in each year. This weighting scheme was introduced to approximate the individual's lifetime income

Table 6.5. Percentage Distribution of LTEAR: Single Population Only[a]

LTEAR[b]	Total	Men	Women
0 - 19.5	13.0	10.9	14.4
19.6 - 41.8	12.7	17.4	9.8
41.9 - 65.2	8.5	7.2	9.3
65.3 - 86.2	5.9	8.7	4.2
86.3 - 106.9	7.4	5.8	8.4
107.0 - 129.5	6.8	6.5	7.0
129.6 - 150.4	5.1	2.9	6.5
150.5 - 168.8	2.5	0.7	3.7
168.9 - 195.5	4.8	2.9	6.0
195.6 - 217.3	6.8	8.0	6.0
217.4 - 238.8	5.4	5.1	5.6
238.9 - 260.7	2.5	0.7	3.7
260.8 - 281.6	4.2	5.1	3.7
281.7 - 302.8	3.1	3.6	2.8
302.9 - 325.1	3.7	5.8	2.3
325.2 - 345.6	2.0	1.4	2.3
345.7 - 361.7	1.7	2.2	1.4
361.8 - 388.3	2.0	2.9	1.4
388.4 - 401.9	0.1	0.7	0.5
401.9+	1.1	1.4	0.9

[a]Totals may not add to 100 because of rounding.

[b]Reported in thousands.

status on the date of retirement. The compounding rate was a simple historical average of the yield on U.S. government securities (low yield) and the annual yield on corporate paper plus the rate of increase of average stock prices (high yield). The historical average series was converted to real terms, since the annual reported earnings were deflated by the consumer price index.

There are obvious problems with the LTEAR measure of lifetime income. First, the selection of an appropriate compounding rate or compounding series is somewhat arbitrary. (The sensitivity of the regression results to the compounding series should be investigated in the future.) Second, LTEAR is based on annual reported earnings to Social Security only; hence, it systematically excludes nonlabor earnings and labor earn-

Table 6.6. Percentage Distribution of FLTEAR by Household Type[a]

FLTEAR[b]	Total	One-Earner	Two-Earner
0 - 40.0	9.2	14.0	3.1
40.1 - 80.3	10.4	14.6	5.0
80.4 - 119.8	8.9	10.8	6.5
119.9 - 160.4	7.7	7.9	7.5
160.5 - 200.0	7.2	6.3	8.5
200.1 - 241.1	8.2	7.8	8.6
241.2 - 281.4	7.4	7.6	7.2
281.5 - 321.9	7.2	5.8	9.0
322.0 - 362.2	8.5	8.3	8.6
362.3 - 402.4	8.5	9.1	7.7
402.5 - 442.1	7.6	5.4	10.4
442.2 - 482.3	3.2	1.4	5.4
482.4 - 522.5	2.1	0.1	3.7
522.6 - 562.3	2.1	0.0	4.6
562.4 - 596.8	0.7	0.0	1.5
596.9 - 637.9	0.4	0.0	1.0
638.0 - 677.5	0.4	0.0	1.0
677.6 - 712.8	0.3	0.0	1.0
712.9 - 730.3	0.1	0.0	0.0
730.4 - 805.2	0.1	0.0	0.0

[a]Totals may not add to 100 because of rounding.

[b]Reported in thousands.

ings above the taxable earnings ceiling. A third problem involves the actual size of the annual taxable earnings reported in the file, which depends on the tax base and types of occupations covered under the law. These policy variables depend on policy decisions that influence the size of the calculated lifetime earnings measure. The last problem with the LTEAR measure is technical in nature. Annual reported earnings for 1937–1950 were not reported annually; rather, the Longitudinal Exact Match File reported a 14-year summary earnings figure. However, the file reports estimated annual quarters of coverage by year for the 1937–1950 time period. The year-specific estimated annual quarters of coverage were used to disaggregate the 1937–1950 summary taxable earnings measure. The disaggregation procedure is described in appendix 3.

In spite of these problems with the LTEAR measure of lifetime earnings, it is still the best measure available, given the information on the worker's earnings history obtained from the Longitudinal Exact Match File. In the context of this study, the most serious shortcoming of the LTEAR measure is the systematic exclusion of nonlabor earnings and earnings above the taxable maximum. The gravity of the problem is challenged, however, by the percentage distribution of the LTEAR and FLTEAR shown in tables 6.5 and 6.6, respectively. But, as a safeguard, a graduated education level variable was included in the regression analysis, since, generally speaking, there is a positive, although not perfect, correlation between income and education levels.

Socioeconomic variables. The SEX, RACE, and EDU dummy variables represent the expected value of the absolute difference in the dependent variable for each beneficiary characteristic, ceteris paribus. The SEX variable was included to monitor the effect, if any, of sex differentials, be they longevity or employment differences, on the extent of redistribution. The dummy variable takes on a value of one when identifying a female. When the annuity counterfactuals reflect survivorship differentials by sex, the coefficient on SEX was expected to be positive.

The RACE variable reflects the race of the family unit, and it was included to determine if race influenced the size of the redistribution component. RACE equals one for nonwhites and zero for whites. RACE was expected to have a negative coefficient when mortality differentials by race were accounted for in the annuity counterfactual.

The EDU variable was included to supplement the earnings measure (LTEAR, FLTEAR), as discussed earlier, and to account for the independent associations of education level on survivorship. Four education classifications were used: EDU1 for persons with up to seven years of education, EDU2 for persons with nine to 11 years of education, EDU3 for high school graduates, and EDU4 for persons with any college education. The coefficients on the EDU variables measure the differential impact of the indicated category and the category of persons with eight years of schooling (the median years of schooling for this age cohort).

The coefficient on EDU1 was expected to be positive without adjusting for education differentials in survivorship but negative if education differentials were introduced into the annuity counterfactual. The sign of the coefficient for EDU2 may be positive or negative. Coefficients on EDU3 and EDU4 were expected to be negative without adjusting for education differentials in survivorship and positive after adjusting for education differentials in survivorship. The sign reversal for EDU3 and EDU4 was expected because education level is inversely related to mortality; hence, the annuity benefits received by persons with high education levels were lower (therefore, their redistribution components larger), ceteris paribus, when survivorship differentials by education level were used to calculate annuity benefits. Education mortality differentials counteract the progressive features of the benefit formula.

Program-worker variables. SERLEN, a continuous variable, is a single number representing the number of years of nonzero reported earnings. The summary measure was constructed by counting the number of years from the year of entry into the labor force to the year of retirement when annual reported earnings were nonzero. Since workers with longer earnings histories pay in more taxes, SERLEN was expected to have a negative coefficient. The coefficient on SERLEN2 was not predicted.

The $RAGER_i$ and $RCOHORT_i$ dummy variables represent the expected value of the absolute difference in the dependent variable for each program-worker characteristic, ceteris paribus. RAGER1, RAGER2, and RAGER3 isolate the importance of retirement age of the beneficiary on the size of the transfer. The retirement age variable (RAGE) itself did not appear on the file, but other variables that were on file were used to construct a retirement age value:

$$\text{RAGE} = \text{LAGE} - (72 - \text{YBEGIN2}) \tag{6.12}$$

where LAGE = the beneficiary's age in 1972 and YBEGIN2 = the year the beneficiary retired. If RAGE equaled 62–64, then a code of one was assigned to RAGER1; if RAGE equaled 66–71, then a code of one was assigned to RAGER2; RAGE greater than 72 was coded as one for RAGER3. The comparison group for this dummy series consisted of persons with a RAGE equal to 65 (i.e., beneficiaries who began receiving benefits at age 65). Previous empirical evidence suggests that RAGER1, RAGER2, and RAGER3 would have negative coefficients. However, RAGER3 may be positive if beneficiaries are collecting special age-72 benefits.

The retirement cohort dummy variables RCOHORT1 and RCOHORT2 measure the significance of the year of retirement in explaining the variation in the size of the transfer component. Persons retiring between 1962 and 1964 were in the earliest cohort labeled RCOHORT1. Persons retiring between 1965 and 1968 were in the middle cohort labeled RCOHORT2. The retirement cohorts dated after 1968 were used as the control group. A positive sign was expected on coefficients for RCOHORT1 and RCOHORT2 because earlier cohorts benefited from the relative immaturity of the program, which made possible extremely low tax rates and frequent increases in benefit levels.

7

New Annuity-Welfare Model Regression Results

The regression results reported in this section are based on the eight models described in chapter 6. There are four permutations of the generalized single model labeled 1, 2, 3, and 4. Recall that the specified models have identical independent variables but different dependent variables measuring the extent of redistribution. Similarly, there are four versions of the married model each having identical independent variables, but, again, different measures of redistribution were used as dependent variables.

In chapter 6, the independent and dependent variables were defined and explained. The regression results presented in this section are organized as follows: 1) findings for the single model, 2) findings for the married model, and 3) summary of findings.

Single Models

The expected signs of the coefficients were discussed in chapter 6 and are summarized in table 7.1. Linear and loglinear models were estimated in addition to the quadratic model; the quadratic variables LTEAR2 and SERLEN2 were found to be jointly significant in all permutations of the generalized single model, although the quadratic terms, when taken separately, were not always found to be statistically significant.[1] Summary statistics for the independent variables employed in the single model appear in table 7.2. As might be expected, there was evidence of correlation between the labor force experience variables (LTEAR and SERLEN). The estimated correlation coefficient was 0.91 and is statistically significant at the 1-percent level. In spite of the strong correlation between the two labor force variables, the estimated coefficients on LTEAR and SERLEN were significantly different from zero at a 1-percent level for all permutations of the single model. At present, there is no obvious solution to this multicollinearity problem without introducing a new statistical problem: specifically, a specification error. However, the construction of a larger, more diverse data set is likely to minimize the collinearity that exists between the labor force variables in this small, relatively homogeneous single data set.

Table 7.1. Single Regression Model Variables and Expected Coefficient Signs for Models 1, 2, 3, and 4 by Survivorship Assumption

Independent variable	Dependent variables in models 1, 2, 3, and 4		
	Gender-merged	Sex-race-distinct	Socioeconomic-adjusted
LTEAR	Negative	Negative	Negative or positive
LTEAR2	Positive	Positive	Negative or positive
SEX	Negative or positive	Positive	Positive
RACE	Negative or positive	Negative	Negative
SERLEN	Negative	Negative	Negative
SERLEN2	Negative or positive	Negative or positive	Negative or positive
RAGER1	Negative	Negative	Negative
RAGER2	Negative	Negative	Negative
RAGER3	Negative	Negative	Negative
RCOHORT1	Positive	Positive	Positive
RCOHORT2	Positive	Positive	Positive
EDU1	Positive	Positive	Negative or positive
EDU2	Negative or positive	Negative or positive	Negative or positive
EDU3	Negative	Negative	Negative or positive
EDU4	Negative	Negative	Negative or positive

Estimation of the Model Using the Annuity Counterfactuals for a Nonindexed, Non-Earnings-Test-Adjusted Insurance Program

As mentioned in chapter 6, this permutation of the single model was estimated to isolate the partial effect of worker-specific characteristics on the percentage of redistribution in the absence of cost-of-living and earnings test adjustments. This narrow definition of the program allows for the isolation of the initial effect of the progressive benefit formula and the minimum benefit provision. The results for model 1 under different survivorship assumptions are reported in table 7.3.

Looking first at the regression results for the model based on the gender-merged survivorship assumption (column 1 in table 7.3), note that all the coefficients for the independent variables have the predicted sign (for those independent variables with predicted signs). The coefficients on the quantitative variables LTEAR and SERLEN are significantly dif-

Table 7.2. Summary Statistics for Independent Variables Employed in the Single Regression Models

Variable	Mean	Standard deviation	Minimum	Maximum
LTEAR	142,211	112,408	0	434,835
SEX	0.61	0.49	0	1
RACE	0.06	0.24	0	1
SERLEN	19.08	9.64	0	36
RAGER1	0.50	0.50	0	1
RAGER2	0.24	0.42	0	1
RAGER3	0.11	0.31	0	1
RCOHORT1	0.32	0.47	0	1
RCOHORT2	0.31	0.46	0	1
EDU1	0.21	0.41	0	1
EDU2	0.10	0.31	0	1
EDU3	0.29	0.46	0	1
EDU4	0.20	0.40	0	1

ferent from zero at a 1-percent level; however, the coefficients for the quadratic terms LTEAR2 and SERLEN2 were not significantly different from zero at a 5-percent level, although they were jointly significant at a 1-percent level. The coefficients on the control variables, RAGER3, RCOHORT1, RCOHORT2, and EDU4, were significantly different from zero at the 1-percent level. The coefficients on SEX, RACE, and EDU2 (variables with unpredicted coefficient signs) were not significantly different from zero.

Column 2 in table 7.3 presents regression results when sex and race survivorship differentials are accounted for in the annuity counterfactuals. All the coefficients, excluding those on RACE and EDU1, have the expected sign. The coefficient on SEX is positive and significantly different from zero at a 1-percent level. Other things equal, women can expect a redistribution component 3.06 percentage points larger than men because of their relatively longer life expectancies, on average. Contrary to expected results, nonwhites, after accounting for their shorter life expectancies, can expect a redistribution component 0.129 percentage points larger than whites, ceteris paribus.

Regression results for model 1 adjusting for socioeconomic differentials in survivorship are presented in column 3 in table 7.3. After accounting for sex, race, marital status, education, and income differentials in survivorship, the OAI program was still found to be progressive; that is, the coefficient on LTEAR is negative and significantly different from zero at a 1-percent level, and, although all coefficients on the education variables are negative, only EDU4 is significantly different from zero at a 1-percent level. Also, the coefficient on RACE is negative, but it is not statistically significant.

The overall effect of accounting for differential life expectancies, in most cases, is slight. Clearly, from the size of the coefficient on SEX, women receive a significantly larger redistribution component when their relatively longer life expectancy is accounted for in their actuarially fair retirement insurance payment.

Estimation of the Model Using the Annuity Counterfactual for an Indexed, Non-Earnings-Test-Adjusted Insurance Program

The dependent variable employed in this version of the single model is the redistribution residual, in percentage terms, assuming the retiree purchased an indexed, non-earnings-test annuity with her accumulated OAI contributions on the date of retirement. The variation in the residual is once again explained by the quadratic model with 12 independent vari-

Table 7.3. Single Regression Results: Model 1 under Different Survivorship Assumptions[a,b]

Variable	Gender-merged	Sex-race-distinct	Socioeconomic-adjusted
	Survivorship probability assumption		
LTEAR	-4.426[a]	-4.166[a]	-4.288[a]
	(4.02)	(3.68)	(3.34)
LTEAR2	0.219[d]	0.173	0.176
	(0.91)	(0.70)	(0.62)
SEX	-0.013	3.063[a]	4.745[a]
	(0.03)	(6.55)	(8.94)
RACE	0.971	0.129	-0.111
	(1.06)	(0.14)	(0.10)
SERLEN	-0.636[a]	-0.626[a]	-0.664[a]
	(5.17)	(4.95)	(4.63)
SERLEN2	0.006[C]	0.006[D]	0.006
	(1.71)	(1.59)	(1.27)
RAGER1	-0.500[d]	-0.354	-0.354
	(0.90)	(0.62)	(0.55)
RAGER2	-0.600[d]	-0.405	-0.323
	(0.98)	(0.65)	(0.46)
RAGER3	-2.126[a]	-2.315[a]	-2.834[a]
	(2.78)	(2.95)	(3.18)
RCOHORT1	9.240[a]	8.975[a]	9.634[a]
	(16.45)	(15.54)	(14.70)
RCOHORT2	6.116[a]	5.980[a]	6.495[a]
	(11.37)	(10.81)	(10.35)
EDU1	0.006	-0.092	-0.394
	(0.01)	(0.13)	(0.51)
EDU2	-0.800	-0.625	-0.482
	(1.0)	(0.76)	(0.52)
EDU3	-0.540[d]	-0.619[d]	-0.573
	(0.86)	(0.96)	(0.78)
EDU4	-2.754[a]	-3.050[a]	-2.535[A]
	(3.89)	(4.18)	(3.07)
Intercept	95.48[a]	93.92[a]	92.45[a]
	(88.19)	(84.38)	(73.21)
R^2	.871	.863	.855
N	353	353	353

[a]t-ratios in parentheses.

[b]Significance levels (uppercase for two-tail tests, lowercase for one-tail tests): A, a – 1%; B, b – 5%; C, c – 10%; D, d – 20%.

ables. The estimated coefficients for model 2 by survivorship assumption appear in table 7.4.

In column 1, coefficients on LTEAR, SERLEN, and SERLEN2 have the correct sign (those with predicted signs) and are significantly different

Table 7.4. Single Regression Results: Model 2 under Different Survivorship Assumptions[a,b]

Variable	Survivorship probability assumption: Gender-merged	Sex-race-distinct	Socioeconomic-adjusted
LTEAR	-4.871[a]	-4.523[a]	-4.884[a]
	(5.48)	(4.99)	(4.31)
LTEAR2	0.334[b]	0.276[c]	0.366[d]
	(1.72)	(1.39)	(1.48)
SEX	-0.072	3.101[a]	5.192[a]
	(0.19)	(8.29)	(11.12)
RACE	0.711	-0.117	-3.487[a]
	(0.96)	(0.16)	(3.71)
SERLEN	-0.662[a]	-0.630[a]	-0.676[a]
	(6.68)	(6.22)	(5.35)
SERLEN2	0.009[A]	0.009[A]	0.007[C]
	(3.14)	(2.90)	(1.95)
RAGER1	-0.054	0.105	0.182
	(0.12)	(0.23)	(0.32)
RAGER2	-0.467[d]	-0.274	-0.116
	(0.95)	(0.55)	(0.19)
RAGER3	-2.415[a]	-2.50[a]	-3.012[a]
	(3.92)	(3.97)	(3.84)
RCOHORT1	6.252[a]	5.90[a]	6.529[a]
	(13.82)	(12.76)	(11.32)
RCOHORT2	4.066[a]	3.876[a]	4.391[a]
	(9.37)	(8.75)	(7.95)
EDU1	0.087	-0.055	-0.303
	(0.16)	(0.10)	(0.44)
EDU2	-0.546	-0.400	-0.309
	(0.85)	(0.61)	(0.38)
EDU3	-0.467[d]	-0.522[d]	-0.535
	(0.92	(1.01)	(0.83)
EDU4	-2.189[a]	-2.41[a]	-2.069[A]
	(3.83)	(4.13)	(2.84)
Intercept	97.55[a]	95.92[a]	94.395[a]
	(111.74)	(107.68)	(84.90)
R^2	.881	.870	.853
N	353	353	353

[a]t-ratios in parentheses.

[b]Significance levels (uppercase for two-tail tests, lowercase for one-tail tests): A, a – 1%; B, b – 5%; C, c – 10%; D, d – 20%.

from zero at a 1-percent level. The coefficient on LTEAR2 has the correct sign and is significantly different from zero at a 5-percent level. All the control variables have the correct sign, and coefficients on RAGER3, RCOHORT1, RCOHORT2, and EDU4 are significantly different from zero at a 1-percent level.

Regression results for model 2 accounting for sex and race differentials in survivorship are shown in column 2 of table 7.4. The coefficients have the expected sign (those with predicted signs) except for RAGER1 and EDU1. Incorporating indexing and survivorship differentials by race and sex into the measure of redistribution produces coefficients on the retirement age variables that are mixed in sign but small in size for RAGER1 and RAGER2. The positive coefficient on RAGER1 suggests that persons will maximize the percentage of redistribution by retiring at age 62 to 64 when lifetime contributions are used to purchase inflation and income insurance. This result may be more reflective of the way annuity benefits were indexed after retirement and the population distribution of the single data set than of the actual structure of the OAI program. This will be discussed further in the last section of the chapter.

Similar results are obtained from the use of socioeconomic-adjusted survivorship probabilities, except the coefficients for SEX and RACE were found to be more statistically significant.

Estimation of the Single Model Using the Annuity Counterfactual for a Nonindexed, Earnings-Test-Adjusted Insurance Program

The nominal annuity benefit employed to calculate the dependent variable was adjusted by the OAI earnings test formula for postretirement earnings in excess of $1,680. The quadratic model had less explanatory power, as reflected by the significantly smaller R^2, because 65 percent of persons with postretirement earnings in excess of $1,680 would have received zero annuity benefits for 1972, resulting in redistribution components equal to 100 percent.

The estimated coefficients in column 1 of table 7.5 have the predicted sign with exception of EDU1; however, only the coefficients for LTEAR, SERLEN, RCOHORT1, and RCOHORT2 are significantly different from zero at a 1-percent level, and the coefficient for RAGER3 is significantly different from zero at a 5-percent level. Nonwhites and persons with up to seven years of education received slightly less redistribution from the OAI program relative to whites and persons with eight years of education, respectively.

Again, the introduction of differentials in survivorship, be they sex-race or socioeconomic, increases the size and significance of the coefficients for RACE and SEX. With the earnings test adjustment of annuity benefits, the level of education variables follows a curious path when mortality differentials are introduced. First, including mortality differentials by sex and race in the annuity counterfactual tends to increase the negative redistributional differential between persons with less than eight or more than 11 years of education relative to persons with eight years of

Table 7.5. Single Regression Results: Model 3 under Different Survivorship Assumptions[a,b]

	Survivorship probability assumption		
Variable	Gender-merged	Sex-race-distinct	Socioeconomic-adjusted
LTEAR	-6.586[a]	-6.208[a]	-6.460[a]
	(3.55)	(3.34)	(3.18)
LTEAR2	0.516[d]	0.411[d]	0.451
	(1.27)	(1.01)	(1.01)
SEX	0.393	3.206[a]	4.789[a]
	(0.51)	(4.18)	(5.72)
RACE	-0.048	-0.852	-1.201
	(0.03)	(0.55)	(0.71)
SERLEN	-0.625[a]	-0.605[a]	-0.619[a]
	(3.02)	(2.91)	(2.73)
SERLEN2	0.012[C]	0.011[C]	0.01[D]
	(1.89)	(1.79)	(1.46)
RAGER1	-0.513	-0.301	-0.291
	(0.55)	(0.32)	(0.28)
RAGER2	-0.317	-0.211	-0.144
	(0.31)	(0.21)	(0.13)
RAGER3	-2.839[b]	-2.918[b]	-3.431[a]
	(2.21)	(2.26)	(2.44)
RCOHORT1	6.50[a]	6.26[a]	6.753[a]
	(6.87)	(6.61)	(6.53)
RCOHORT2	3.109[a]	2.993[a]	3.343[a]
	(3.44)	(3.30)	(3.37)
EDU1	-0.295	-0.482	-0.824
	(0.26)	(0.43)	(0.67)
EDU2	-0.072	-0.069	0.233
	(0.05)	(0.05)	(0.16)
EDU3	-0.785	-0.802	-0.736
	(0.74)	(0.75)	(0.63)
EDU4	-1.783[c]	-2.133[b]	-1.689[D]
	(1.50)	(1.78)	(1.29)
Intercept	97.93[a]	96.42[a]	95.11[a]
	(53.78)	(52.81)	(47.69)
R^2	.628	.629	.637
N	353	353	353

[a]t-ratios in parentheses.

[b]Significance levels (uppercase for two-tail tests, lowercase for one-tail tests): A, a – 1%; B, b – 5%; C, c – 10%; D, d – 20%.

education. But there is a slight narrowing of the redistributional differential between persons with nine to 11 years of education relative to persons with only eight years of schooling when sex and race differentials are reflected in mortality rates. Further disaggregation of mortality rates by marital status, income, and education levels tends to strengthen the tendency of the sex and race adjustments for EDU1 only. For all other education categories, the redistributional differential is narrowed, and, for EDU2, the differential sign is positive. This suggests that the earnings test slightly weakens the program's progressivity, which is consistent with the smaller coefficients for LTEAR in columns 2 and 3 relative to column 1.

Estimation of the Single Model Using the Annuity Counterfactual for an Indexed, Earnings-Test-Adjusted Insurance Program

Similar results are obtained with this final permutation of the generalized single model, in which the dependent variable is based on an annuity counterfactual promising to pay a real stream of benefits for the life of the annuitant and some or all benefits are forfeited if postretirement earnings exceed $1,680. (The fraction forfeited depends on the size of the annuity benefit and the amount of earnings over $1,680.) The regression results are reported in table 7.6.

With the notable exception of the coefficients for the education variables EDU1 and EDU2 in column 1, RAGER1 and EDU1 in column 2, and RAGER1 in column 3, all the coefficients have the expected sign. In column 1, the coefficients on EDU1 and EDU2 are negative and positive, respectively, indicating that persons with less than eight years of education received less, and persons with nine to 11 years of education received more, redistribution per dollar of OAI benefit relative to persons with eight years of schooling. The redistributional differential generally increases with the incorporation of disaggregated mortality differentials.

Comparison of Models 1, 2, and 4 Controlling for Differential Survivorship Probabilities

In the previous subsections, the effect of differential mortality on the estimated coefficients across permutations of the generalized single model was examined. This subsection focuses on the effect of different program features on the size and sign of the estimated parameters, holding the survivorship assumption constant. The coefficient estimates for models 1, 2, and 4 for the gender-merged and socioeconomic-adjusted survivorship probability assumptions are reproduced in tables 7.7 and 7.8, respectively.

Looking first at the coefficients in table 7.7, note that benefit indexing and earnings test adjustments, when accounted for in the annuity counterfactual, do have an effect on the relationship between the independent and dependent variables as reflected in the estimated coefficients. For

Table 7.6. Single Regression Results: Model 4 under Different Survivorship Assumptions[a,b]

Variable	Survivorship probability assumption		
	Gender-merged	Sex-race-distinct	Socioeconomic-adjusted
LTEAR	-6.589[a]	-6.101[a]	-6.639[a]
	(4.11)	(3.87)	(3.65)
LTEAR2	0.528[c]	0.439[d]	0.532[D]
	(1.51)	(1.17)	(1.34)
SEX	0.284	3.164[a]	5.156[a]
	(0.43)	(4.87)	(6.87)
RACE	-0.103	-0.943	-4.362[a]
	(0.08)	(0.72)	(2.89)
SERLEN	-0.661[a]	-0.628[a]	-0.649[a]
	(3.70)	(3.57)	(3.20)
SERLEN2	0.014[A]	0.014[A]	0.012[B]
	(2.67)	(2.62)	(1.95)
RAGER1	-0.129	0.063	0.149
	(0.16)	(0.08)	(0.16)
RAGER2	-0.283	-0.227	-0.074
	(0.32)	(0.26)	(0.07)
RAGER3	-3.051[a]	-3.044[a]	-3.576[a]
	(2.75)	(2.79)	(2.83)
RCOHORT1	3.851[a]	3.598[a]	3.989[a]
	(4.72)	(4.48)	(4.30)
RCOHORT2	1.435[b]	1.331[b]	1.598[b]
	(1.84)	(1.73)	(1.80)
EDU1	-0.136	-0.392	-0.701
	(0.14)	(0.41)	(0.64)
EDU2	0.115	0.138	0.293
	(0.10)	(0.12)	(0.22)
EDU3	-0.685	-0.701	-0.711
	(0.75)	(0.72)	(0.68)
EDU4	-1.417[c]	-1.723[b]	-1.441[a]
	(1.38)	(1.70)	(1.23)
Intercept	99.747[a]	98.229[a]	96.934[a]
	(63.42)	(63.51)	(54.26)
R^2	.624	.624	.636
N	353	353	353

[a]t-ratios in parentheses.

[b]Significance levels (uppercase for two-tail tests, lowercase for one-tail tests): A, a – 1%; B, b – 5%; C, c – 10%; D, d – 20%.

instance, the coefficient on the lifetime earnings measure increases in absolute size with the introduction of indexing and earnings test adjustments into the annuity counterfactual. At first blush, this evidence would tend to suggest that the program becomes more progressive as the annuity

Table 7.7. Single Regression Results: Comparison of Models 1, 2, and 4 Using Gender-Merged Survivorship Probabilities

Variable	Model 1	Model 2	Model 4
LTEAR	-4.426	-4.871	-6.589
LTEAR2	0.219	0.334	0.528
SEX	-0.013	-0.072	0.284
RACE	0.971	0.711	-0.103
SERLEN	-0.636	-0.662	-0.661
SERLEN2	0.006	0.009	0.014
RAGER1	-0.500	-0.054	-0.129
RAGER2	-0.600	-0.467	-0.283
RAGER3	-2.126	-2.415	-3.051
RCOHORT1	9.240	6.252	3.851
RCOHORT2	6.116	4.066	1.435
EDU1	0.006	0.087	-0.136
EDU2	-0.800	-0.546	0.115
EDU3	-0.540	-0.467	-0.685
EDU4	-2.754	-2.189	-1.417
Intercept	95.48	97.55	99.747
R^2	.871	.881	.628

counterfactual more closely approximates the OAI program. However, this generalization may be too strong in light of the observed pattern on the coefficients for LTEAR2 and the education variables. The coefficient for LTEAR2 enters with a positive sign in column 1 and increases across the model, offsetting the strength of the negative coefficient on LTEAR. Likewise, the coefficients on the education variable show a weakening of progressivity across the models. The coefficient estimates for EDU1 across models 1 and 4 show a withering away of the redistributional gains for persons with up to seven years of education relative to persons with eight years of schooling. The redistributional losses associated with education levels of 13 or more years of education are reduced, and for education levels nine to 11, the loss not only diminishes but becomes a gain when the earnings test is added to the annuity counterfactual.

A few additional patterns across models are worth mentioning. The sign change on the estimated coefficient for SEX with the accounting for the earnings test suggests that single women were more likely to continue working after retirement; as a result, women tended to have slightly larger redistribution components. The pattern on the coefficient for RACE, on the other hand, suggests that the redistributional gains of nonwhites are reduced under indexing; with the addition of an earnings test, nonwhites

Table 7.8. Single Regression Results: Comparison of Models 1, 2, and 4 Using Socioeconomic-Adjusted Survivorship Probabilities

Variable	Model 1	Model 2	Model 4
LTEAR	-4.288	-4.884	-6.639
LTEAR2	0.176	0.366	0.532
SEX	4.745	5.192	5.156
RACE	-0.111	-3.487	-4.362
SERLEN	-0.664	-0.676	-0.649
SERLEN2	0.006	0.007	0.012
RAGER1	-0.354	0.182	0.149
RAGER2	-0.323	-0.116	-0.074
RAGER3	-2.834	-3.012	-3.576
RCOHORT1	9.634	6.529	3.989
RCOHORT2	6.495	4.391	1.598
EDU1	-0.394	-0.303	-0.701
EDU2	-0.482	-0.309	0.293
EDU3	-0.573	-0.535	-0.711
EDU4	-2.535	-2.069	-1.441
Intercept	92.45	94.395	96.934
R^2	.855	.853	.636

receive slightly less redistribution when compared to their white counterparts. The last, and perhaps the most dramatic, pattern to be mentioned concerns the estimated coefficients on the retirement cohort variables, RCOHORT1 and RCOHORT2. The redistribution gains for persons retiring in 1962–1965 and 1966–1968 relative to the 1969–1972 retirement cohort consistently diminish across models.

Similar results are observed using socioeconomic-adjusted probabilities (see table 7.8). Note that females received slightly more redistribution from an indexed system relative to males, again, because of their longer life expectancies. Alternatively, nonwhites are made significantly worse off, in terms of the reduced share of redistribution from an indexed system, relative to whites because of race differentials in survivorship (compare columns 1 and 2).

Married Models

Reported regression results are based on the estimation of four permutations of the generalized married quadratic model. Linear and loglinear models were estimated, but the quadratic variables FLTEAR2, SERLEN2, and _SERLEN2 were found to be jointly, although only FLTEAR2 was found to be separately, significant in all permutations of the generalized model.[2] The expected signs for all 24 independent variables are summarized in table 7.9, and summary statistics for each independent variable appear in table 7.10. There was evidence of correlation between the service length variables within a household, but collinearity was not a problem between the lifetime earnings measure (FLTEAR) and service length variables (SERLEN, _SERLEN). The correlation coefficient on the service length variables SERLEN and _SERLEN was relatively small, 0.33, but significantly different from zero at the 5-percent level.

Estimation of the Model Using the Annuity Counterfactual for a Nonindexed, Non-Earnings-Test-Adjusted Insurance Program

As discussed in chapter 6, the annuity counterfactual used to determine the percentage of redistribution was based on the assumption that the retirement candidate purchased a life annuity that promised payment of a nominal stream of income for life and that guaranteed the invariance of the benefit payment to postretirement earnings. The quadratic model with 24 independent variables was estimated to isolate the partial effect of household-specific characteristics on the percentage of redistribution for the household. The results for model 5 under different survivorship assumptions are presented in table 7.11.

Table 7.9. Married Regression Model Variables and Expected Coefficient Signs for Models 5, 6, 7, and 8 by Survivorship Assumption

Independent variable	Dependent variables in models 5, 6, 7, and 8		
	Gender-merged	Sex-race-distinct	Socioeconomic-adjusted
FLTEAR	Negative	Negative	Negative or positive
FLTEAR2	Positive	Positive	Negative or positive
RACE	Negative or positive	Negative	Negative
SERLEN	Negative	Negative	Negative
_SERLEN	Negative	Negative	Negative
SERLEN2	Negative or positive	Negative or positive	Negative or positive
_SERLEN2	Negative or positive	Negative or positive	Negative or positive
RAGER1	Negative	Negative	Negative
RAGER2	Negative	Negative	Negative
RAGER3	Negative or positive	Negative or positive	Negative or positive
_RAGER1	Negative	Negative	Negative
_RAGER2	Negative	Negative	Negative
RCOHORT1	Positive	Positive	Positive
RCOHORT2	Positive	Positive	Positive
_RCOHORT1	Positive	Positive	Positive
_RCOHORT2	Positive	Positive	Positive
EDU1	Positive	Positive	Negative or positive
EDU2	Negative or positive	Negative or positive	Negative or positive
EDU3	Negative	Negative	Negative or positive
EDU4	Negative	Negative	Negative or positive
_EDU1	Positive	Positive	Negative or positive
_EDU2	Negative or positive	Negative or positive	Negative or positive
_EDU3	Negative	Negative	Negative or positive
_EDU4	Negative	Negative	Negative or positive

In the regression for the gender-merged survivorship probabilities (column 1), all independent variables have the predicted sign, with the exception of SERLEN, EDU1, EDU4, _EDU1, _EDU3, and _EDU4. Of those variables with the predicted sign, only FLTEAR, FLTEAR2,

Table 7.10. Summary Statistics for Independent Variables Employed in the Married Regression Models

Variable	Mean	Standard deviation	Minimum	Maximum
FLTEAR	241,996	155,621	0	805,200
RACE	0.02	0.13	0	1.00
SERLEN	6.43	8.41	0	35.00
_SERLEN	21.50	10.14	0	36.00
RAGER1	0.76	0.43	0	1
RAGER2	0.11	0.31	0	1
RAGER3	0.10	0.31	0	1
_RAGER1	0.42	0.49	0	1
_RAGER2	0.26	0.44	0	1
RCOHORT1	0.26	0.44	0	1
RCOHORT2	0.29	0.45	0	1
_RCOHORT1	0.36	0.48	0	1
_RCOHORT2	0.31	0.46	0	1
EDU1	0.18	0.38	0	1
EDU2	0.17	0.38	0	1
EDU3	0.25	0.44	0	1
EDU4	0.16	0.36	0	1
_EDU1	0.23	0.42	0	1
_EDU2	0.16	0.37	0	1
_EDU3	0.17	0.38	0	1
_EDU4	0.15	0.36	0	1

_RAGER1, RCOHORT1, RCOHORT2, _RCOHORT1, and _RCOHORT2 have estimated coefficients that are significantly different from zero at a 5-percent level. And of those variables with an unpredicted sign,

Table 7.11. Married Regression Results: Model 5 under Different Survivorship Assumptions[a,b]

Variable	Survivorship probability assumption		
	Gender-merged	Sex-race-distinct	Socioeconomic-adjusted
FLTEAR	-4.071[a]	-3.994[a]	-4.002[A]
	(26.81)	(26.72)	(26.73)
FLTEAR2	0.154[a]	0.152[a]	0.157[A]
	(5.80)	(5.82)	(6.00)
RACE	-0.305	-0.718[d]	0.977[a]
	(0.53)	(1.27)	(1.73)
SERLEN	0.007	0.008	0.008
	(0.25)	(0.29)	(0.29)
_SERLEN	-0.043[c]	-0.042[c]	-0.042[c]
	(1.49)	(1.51)	(1.49)
SERLEN2	0.000	0.000	0.000
	(0.01)	(0.01)	(0.07)
_SERLEN2	0.001	0.001	0.001
	(0.95)	(0.96)	(1.01)
RAGER1	-0.056	0.038	-0.044
	(0.25)	(0.17)	(0.20)
RAGER2	-0.429[c]	-0.460[c]	-0.528[b]
	(1.43)	(1.55)	(1.78)
RAGER3	0.774[A]	0.779[A]	0.849[A]
	(2.93)	(3.05)	(3.32)
_RAGER1	-0.534[a]	-0.528[a]	-0.546[a]
	(3.05)	(3.37)	(3.16)
_RAGER2	-0.291[c]	-0.273[c]	-0.295[c]
	(1.50)	(1.43)	(1.54)
RCOHORT1	1.874[a]	1.746[a]	1.788[a]
	(8.39)	(7.94)	(8.12)
RCOHORT2	1.493[a]	1.421[a]	1.444[a]
	(7.51)	(7.26)	(7.37)
_RCOHORT1	5.404[a]	5.394[a]	5.359[a]
	(24.67)	(25.01)	(24.82)
_RCOHORT2	3.556[a]	3.544[a]	3.536[a]
	(17.65)	(17.87)	(17.80)
EDU1	-0.126	-0.118	-0.301
	(0.52)	(0.49)	(1.26)
EDU2	-0.201	-0.180	0.084
	(0.84)	(0.77)	(0.36)
EDU3	-0.088	-0.070	0.091
	(0.38)	(0.31)	(0.40)
EDU4	0.203	0.223	0.969[A]
	(0.74)	(0.82)	(3.58)
_EDU1	-0.107	-0.095	-0.038
	(0.49)	(0.44)	(0.18)

[a]t-ratios in parentheses.

[b]Significance levels (uppercase for two-tail tests, lowercase for one-tail tests): A, a – 1%; B, b – 5%; C, c – 10%; D, d – 20%.

Table 7.11. (contd.)

_EDU2	0.332[D]	0.317[D]	0.309[D]
	(1.42)	(1.37)	(1.34)
_EDU3	0.047	0.044	0.055
	(0.19)	(0.18)	(0.23)
_EDU4	0.051	0.043	0.055
	(0.19)	(0.16)	(0.20)
Intercept	92.560[a]	92.655[a]	92.520[a]
	(208.47)	(211.94)	(211.35)
R^2	.849	.848	.846
N	1,394	1,394	1,394

only the coefficient for RAGER3 is significantly different from zero at a 1-percent level.

Of the six quantitative variables, only FLTEAR and FLTEAR2 explain a significant amount of the variation of the percentage of redistribution around its mean. As expected, the estimated coefficients on FLTEAR and FLTEAR2 are negative and positive, respectively, but, when taken together, there exists a negative association between the family measure of the percentage of redistribution and family lifetime earnings. The estimated coefficients for the education variables for the husband and wife are small, and they were found to be statistically insignificant, separately and jointly. However, the signs on the education variable coefficients, especially on EDU1, EDU4, _EDU1, and _EDU4, challenge the progressivity conclusion based exclusively on the overall sign of the coefficient on the family lifetime earnings measures.

The interpretation of the other independent variables is straightforward and consistent with earlier discussions for the single models, with the exception of RAGER3. The coefficient for RAGER3 is positive and statistically significant. This suggests that households in which the woman retired after age 71 received a redistribution component that was 0.774 percentage points larger than households in which the woman retired at age 65, ceteris paribus.

Next, looking at regression results in column 2, there are only minor changes in the estimated coefficients after accounting for mortality differentials by sex and race. The coefficient for RACE, while small and statistically insignificant, indicates that nonwhite households received slightly less redistribution relative to white households. The coefficient for RACE is, however, only slightly larger after adjustments are made for race differentials in survivorship. Perhaps, though, the most curious finding is the sign switching on the coefficient for RAGER1 after introducing sex and race differentials in survivorship. In that case, households in which women retired before age 65 and after age 71 received slightly larger redistribution components relative to households in which women retired at age 65.

The regression results for model 5 after accounting for socioeconomic differentials in survivorship are presented in column 3 of table 7.11. The coefficients for the following variables are significantly different from zero at a 5-percent level: FLTEAR, FLTEAR2, RACE, RAGER2, RAGER3, _RAGER1, RCOHORT1, RCOHORT2, _RCOHORT1, _RCOHORT2, and EDU4. Two interesting results should be noted. The coefficient for RACE is positive and significantly different from zero at a 1-percent level after controlling for race, sex, marital status, education, and income differentials in survivorship. Also, the coefficient for EDU4 is positive and significantly different from zero at a 1-percent level. That is, households in which the woman has some college education received a redistribution component that was approximately 0.97 percentage points larger than households in which the woman had eight years of education.

Comparisons of the results across survivorship assumptions suggest that for married households aggregate results do not significantly change, except for RACE, RAGER1, and EDU4, with mortality rate disaggregation.

Estimation of the Model Using the Annuity Counterfactual for an Indexed, Non-Earnings-Test-Adjusted Insurance Program

The dependent variable employed in this version of the married model is based on an annuity counterfactual promising a real stream of benefits for the life of the annuitants. The variation in the dependent variable is once again explained by the quadratic model with 24 independent variables. The estimated coefficients by survivorship assumption appear in table 7.12.

Regression results for model 6 based on gender-merged survivorship probabilities are reported in column 1. The coefficients for FLTEAR, FLTEAR2, RAGER2, RAGER3, _RAGER1, _RAGER2, RCOHORT1, RCOHORT2, _RCOHORT1, and _RCOHORT2 are significantly different from zero at a 5-percent level, and they enter with the predicted sign (for those with a predicted sign). When the annuity promises to pay a fixed real benefit level for the life of the annuitants, the household received slightly more redistribution if the woman elected to retire prior to age 65, as reflected by the coefficient for RAGER1. The redistribution gains are larger yet for the household in which the woman retired after age 71, everything else equal.

The results for the education dummy variables are mixed, and all eight coefficients are small. According to the signs of the coefficients for

Table 7.12. Married Regression Results: Model 6 under Different Survivorship Assumptions[a,b]

Variable	Survivorship probability assumption		
	Gender-merged	Sex-race-distinct	Socioeconomic-adjusted
FLTEAR	-3.894[a]	-3.793[a]	-3.791[A]
	(31.03)	(30.79)	(30.90)
FLTEAR2	0.190[a]	0.185[a]	0.190[A]
	(8.62)	(8.56)	(8.84)
RACE	-0.197	-0.606[c]	1.097[a]
	(0.42)	(1.30)	(2.37)
SERLEN	0.006	0.007	0.007
	(0.27)	(0.32)	(0.32)
_SERLEN	-0.031[c]	-0.031[c]	-0.030[c]
	(1.30)	(1.32)	(1.28)
SERLEN2	0.000	0.000	0.000
	(0.01)	(0.04)	(0.10)
_SERLEN2	0.000	0.000	0.001
	(0.82)	(0.83)	(0.87)
RAGER1	0.081	0.202[d]	0.117
	(0.44)	(1.12)	(0.65)
RAGER2	-0.473[b]	-0.518[b]	-0.565[a]
	(1.90)	(2.12)	(2.32)
RAGER3	1.113[A]	1.119[A]	1.167[A]
	(5.19)	(5.32)	(5.57)
_RAGER1	-0.394[a]	-0.473[a]	-0.435[a]
	(2.72)	(3.32)	(3.08)
_RAGER2	-0.306[b]	-0.277[b]	-0.297[b]
	(1.90)	(1.75)	(1.88)
RCOHORT1	1.056[a]	0.877[a]	0.929[a]
	(5.72)	(4.84)	(5.15)
RCOHORT2	0.965[a]	0.868[a]	0.891[a]
	(5.87)	(5.38)	(5.55)
_RCOHORT1	3.691[a]	3.764[a]	3.711[a]
	(20.39)	(21.18)	(20.97)
_RCOHORT2	2.345[a]	2.379[a]	2.357[a]
	(14.08)	(14.56)	(14.48)
EDU1	-0.084	-0.074	-0.270[D]
	(0.42)	(0.38)	(1.37)
EDU2	-0.148	-0.123	0.151
	(0.75)	(0.64)	(0.78)
EDU3	-0.045	-0.023	0.159
	(0.23)	(0.16)	(0.85)
EDU4	0.140	0.168	1.054[A]
	(0.62)	(0.75)	(4.75)
_EDU1	-0.138	-0.122	-0.071
	(0.76)	(0.69)	(0.40)

[a]t-ratios in parentheses.

[b]Significance levels (uppercase for two-tail tests, lowercase for one-tail tests): A, a – 1%; B, b – 5%; C, c – 10%; D, d – 20%.

Table 7.12. (contd.)

_EDU2	0.266[b]	0.249[b]	0.239[b]
	(1.37)	(1.31)	(1.26)
_EDU3	0.058	0.054	0.064
	(0.29)	(0.27)	(0.33)
_EDU4	0.020	0.006	0.009
	(0.09)	(0.03)	(0.04)
Intercept	94.233[a]	94.302[a]	94.167[a]
	(256.81)	(261.83)	(262.50)
R^2	.848	.846	.845
N	1,394	1,394	1,394

EDU1, EDU2, EDU3, and EDU4, households received slightly less redistribution when the female member had less than eight or nine to 12 years of education, whereas households received slightly more redistribution when the female member had some college education, relative to households where the female member had eight years of schooling. Turning to the comparable coefficients for the male member, households in which the male member had nine or more years of schooling received slightly larger redistribution components (although the marginal gain decreased with extra years of schooling), whereas the opposite was true for households in which the male member had less than eight years of education, when compared to households in which the male member had eight years of schooling, ceteris paribus.

Introducing disaggregated survivorship probabilities does change some of the basic findings under the gender-merged assumption. First, looking at the sex-race disaggregated assumption in column 2 of table 7.12, the changes are relatively minor and confined to race and sex-distinct dummy variables. The race coefficient is slightly more negative, as are the coefficients for RAGER2 and _RAGER1. Alternatively, the redistributional gains to households in which the female retired prior to age 65 were slightly increased; however, the redistributional gains to households in which the female retired prior to 1969 were slightly reduced.

When survivorship probabilities are further disaggregated by marital status, education, and income, the coefficient estimates affected are for the variables RACE, EDU1, EDU2, EDU3, EDU4, _EDU1, and _EDU4. Clearly, the most dramatic change pertains to the coefficient for RACE, which, in column 3, is positive and significantly different from zero at a 1-percent level. On average, nonwhite households received redistribution components 1.097 percentage points larger than white households, ceteris paribus.

Similarly speaking, the accounting for education differentials in survivorship, in addition to sex differentials, affects the estimated coefficients for EDU1, EDU2, EDU3, EDU4, _EDU1, and _EDU4. The household measure of redistribution was smaller if the female member had less than eight years of education, but it was larger if the female member had more than eight years of education. The coefficients on EDU1, EDU2, and EDU3 were small; however, the coefficient for EDU4 was positive and significantly different from zero at the 1-percent level. The size of the redistributional loss for households in which the male member had less than eight years of schooling decreased when sex and education differentials in survivorship were introduced. However, the estimated coefficients for _EDU2 and _EDU3 were remarkably stable under different survivorship assumptions.

Estimation of the Married Model Using the Annuity Counterfactual for the Nonindexed, Earnings-Test-Adjusted Insurance Program

The dependent variable was constructed using the nominal annuity benefit counterfactual adjusted by the OAI earnings test formula. The explanatory power of the generalized married model, as reflected by the smaller R^2, is significantly weakened by the larger deviations in the redistribution measure for observations affected by the earnings test. Approximately 10 percent of the married households were affected by the earnings test.

All the estimated coefficients in column 1 of table 7.13 have the predicted sign, with the exception of SERLEN, SERLEN2, EDU1, EDU4, _EDU1, _EDU3, and _EDU4. Of the coefficients with the correct sign, the estimates for FLTEAR, FLTEAR2, _RAGER2, RCOHORT1, RCOHORT2, _RCOHORT1, and _RCOHORT2 are significantly different from zero at the 5-percent level. Only one of the coefficients with an unpredicted sign is statistically significant at a 5- or 1-percent level, RAGER3. The coefficients on the service length variables (SERLEN, _SERLEN, SERLEN2, and _SERLEN2) have mixed signs and are statistically insignificant, separately and jointly.

The introduction of disaggregated survivorship probabilities, either by sex and race or by sex, race, marital status, income, and education, does not significantly affect the aggregate results, with the notable exception of RACE and the education variables.

Estimation of the Married Model Using the Annuity Counterfactual for an Indexed, Earnings-Test-Adjusted Insurance Program

The final permutation of the generalized married model was estimated to explain the variation in the redistribution component calculated using an

Table 7.13. Married Regression Results: Model 7 under Different Survivorship Assumptions[a,b]

Variable	Survivorship probability assumption		
	Gender-merged	Sex-race-distinct	Socioeconomic-adjusted
FLTEAR	-3.949[a]	-3.874[a]	-3.884[A]
	(16.18)	(16.16)	(16.28)
FLTEAR2	0.176[a]	0.176[a]	0.179[A]
	(4.11)	(4.13)	(4.28)
RACE	-0.358	-0.770[d]	0.920[d]
	(0.39)	(0.85)	(1.02)
SERLEN	0.007	0.008	0.007
	(0.16)	(0.18)	(0.17)
_SERLEN	-0.023	-0.023	-0.022
	(0.51)	(0.50)	(0.49)
SERLEN2	-0.001	-0.001	-0.001
	(0.69)	(0.70)	(0.72)
_SERLEN2	0.001	0.001	0.001
	(0.61)	(0.60)	(0.62)
RAGER1	-0.224	-0.129	-0.201
	(0.63)	(0.37)	(0.58)
RAGER2	-0.122	-0.149	-0.207
	(0.25)	(0.31)	(0.44)
RAGER3	3.40[A]	3.362[A]	3.405[A]
	(8.15)	(8.21)	(8.35)
_RAGER1	-0.354[d]	-0.399[c]	-0.362[c]
	(1.26)	(1.44)	(1.31)
_RAGER2	-0.601[b]	-0.578[b]	-0.594[b]
	(1.92)	(1.88)	(1.94)
RCOHORT1	1.748[a]	1.631[a]	1.680[a]
	(4.87)	(4.62)	(4.78)
RCOHORT2	1.373[a]	1.308[a]	1.337[a]
	(4.30)	(4.17)	(4.28)
_RCOHORT1	3.794[a]	3.803[a]	3.784[a]
	(10.77)	(11.00)	(10.99)
_RCOHORT2	1.980[a]	1.989[a]	1.998[a]
	(6.11)	(6.25)	(6.31)
EDU1	-0.236	-0.226	-0.410
	(0.60)	(0.59)	(1.07)
EDU2	-0.319	-0.297	-0.043
	(0.83)	(0.79)	(0.11)
EDU3	-0.396[d]	-0.370[d]	-0.216
	(1.07)	(1.02)	(0.60)
EDU4	0.238	0.249	0.927[B]
	(0.54)	(0.57)	(2.15)
_EDU1	-0.680[b]	-0.657[b]	-0.602[C]
	(1.92)	(1.89)	(1.74)

[a]t-ratios in parentheses.

[b]Significance levels (uppercase for two-tail tests, lowercase for one-tail tests): A, a – 1%; B, b – 5%; C, c – 10%; D, d – 20%.

Table 7.13. (contd.)

_EDU2	0.453[b]	0.435[b]	0.429[b]
	(1.20)	(1.18)	(1.17)
_EDU3	0.000	-0.003	0.020
	(0.0)	(0.01)	(0.05)
_EDU4	0.616[c]	0.603[c]	0.598[c]
	(1.41)	(1.41)	(1.40)
Intercept	93.934[a]	94.001[a]	93.856[a]
	(131.60)	(134.12)	(134.51)
R^2	.619	.618	.619
N	1,394	1,394	1,394

indexed annuity counterfactual adjusted by the OAI earnings test formula. The regression results are reported in table 7.14 by survivorship assumption.

Based on the gender-merged assumption, the estimated coefficients for FLTEAR, FLTEAR2, RAGER3, _RAGER2, RCOHORT1, RCOHORT2, _RCOHORT1, and _RCOHORT2 have the predicted sign (for those with a predicted sign) and were significantly different from zero at a 5-percent level (see column 1). The coefficient for _EDU1 was significantly different from zero at a 5-percent level, but it did not have the predicted sign. Again, the coefficients for the education variables were mixed and statistically insignificant, separately (with the exception of _EDU1) but not jointly.

Disaggregating survivorship probabilities by race and sex resulted in only modest changes in the coefficient estimates for RACE and RAGER1 (see column 2). Further disaggregation of survivorship probabilities by marital status, income, and education also resulted in only modest changes in the parameter estimates. The estimates for model 8 employing socio-economic-adjusted survivorship probabilities are presented in column 3 of table 7.14. The coefficient for RACE does not have the predicted sign and is significantly different from zero at a 10-percent level. The coefficient for EDU1 is generally more negative and that for _EDU1 less negative as survivorship probabilities are more disaggregated. The coefficient for EDU2 turns positive when mortality differentials by marital status, income, and education are included, and, more importantly, the coefficient for EDU4 is positive and significantly different from zero at a 1-percent level.

Comparison of Models 5, 6, and 8 Controlling for Differential Survivorship Probabilities

In this subsection, the effect of different program features on the size and sign of the estimated coefficients will be investigated under the same sur-

Table 7.14. Married Regression Results: Model 8 under Different Survivorship Assumptions[a,b]

	Survivorship probability assumption		
Variable	Gender-merged	Sex-race-distinct	Socioeconomic-adjusted
FLTEAR	-3.786[a] (18.22)	-3.688[a] (18.17)	-3.689[A] (18.36)
FLTEAR2	0.205[a] (5.64)	0.200[a] (5.64)	0.206[A] (5.85)
RACE	-0.234 (0.30)	-0.639 (0.83)	1.059[c] (1.40)
SERLEN	0.005 (0.14)	0.006 (0.16)	0.005 (0.15)
_SERLEN	-0.012 (0.32)	-0.012 (0.31)	-0.010 (0.28)
SERLEN2	-0.001 (0.68)	-0.001 (0.68)	-0.001 (0.70)
_SERLEN2	0.000 (0.45)	0.000 (0.44)	0.000 (0.44)
RAGER1	-0.039 (0.13)	0.081 (0.27)	0.007 (0.02)
RAGER2	-0.221 (0.54)	-0.261 (0.65)	-0.299 (0.75)
RAGER3	3.262[A] (9.19)	3.226[A] (9.30)	3.240[A] (9.43)
_RAGER1	-0.234[d] (0.97)	-0.308[c] (1.32)	-0.270[d] (1.16)
_RAGER2	-0.525[b] (1.97)	-0.492[b] (1.89)	-0.505[b] (1.96)
RCOHORT1	0.949[a] (3.10)	0.785[a] (2.63)	0.844[a] (2.85)
RCOHORT2	0.876[a] (3.22)	0.788[a] (2.97)	0.817[a] (3.11)
_RCOHORT1	2.344[a] (7.82)	2.433[a] (8.31)	2.401[a] (8.28)
_RCOHORT2	1.046[a] (3.79)	1.098[a] (4.08)	1.098[a] (4.12)
EDU1	-0.171 (0.51)	-0.160 (0.49)	-0.355 (1.10)
EDU2	-0.240 (0.74)	-0.215 (0.67)	0.050 (0.16)
EDU3	-0.268[d] (0.85)	-0.241 (0.78)	-0.066 (0.21)
EDU4	0.170 (0.45)	0.188 (0.51)	0.998[A] (2.75)
_EDU1	-0.606[b] (2.02)	-0.579[b] (1.97)	-0.529[C] (1.82)

[a]t-ratios in parentheses.

[b]Significance levels (uppercase for two-tail tests, lowercase for one-tail tests): A, a – 1%; B, b – 5%; C, c – 10%; D, d – 20%.

Table 7.14. (contd.)

_EDU2	0.375	0.352	0.345
	(1.17)	(1.13)	(1.11)
_EDU3	0.040	0.036	0.060
	(0.12)	(0.11)	(0.19)
_EDU4	0.506[c]	0.485[c]	0.469[D]
	(1.36)	(1.34)	(1.31)
Intercept	95.34[a]	95.379[a]	95.230[a]
	(156.93)	(160.70)	(162.03)
R^2	.611	.610	.612
N	1,394	1,394	1,394

vivorship assumption. In table 7.15, the coefficients for models 5, 6, and 8 using gender-merged survivorship probabilities are presented. Comparisons of models 5, 6, and 8 findings based on socioeconomic-adjusted survivorship probabilities appear in table 7.16.

Most of the coefficient estimates shown in table 7.15 are remarkably stable across program features, but some important trends are observed. First, the combined effect of FLTEAR and FLTEAR2 shows a weakening of the program's progressivity when the annuity counterfactual includes indexing and the earnings test. Second, the coefficient for RAGER1 is positive when benefit indexing is included in the annuity counterfactual but becomes negative when, in addition to indexing, the earnings test is adopted. However, the coefficient for RAGER3 becomes progressively larger as the annuity counterfactual more closely replicates the OAI program. Looking at the comparable variables for men, the coefficient for _RAGER1 decreases in size, whereas the coefficient for _RAGER2 increases in size, as additional program features are included in the annuity counterfactual. Third, the coefficients for the retirement cohort variables (RCOHORT1, RCOHORT2, _RCOHORT1, _RCOHORT2) systematically decrease across the model variations. Similar results, although not identical measures, are observed in table 7.16.

Summary of Regression Findings

Lifetime Earnings Variables

For all permutations of the single and married models, the estimated coefficient for the household measure of lifetime earnings (LTEAR, FLTEAR) is negative and significant at a 1-percent level. This suggests that, when all other household characteristics were held constant, households with higher lifetime earnings received smaller redistribution com-

Table 7.15. Married Regression Results: Comparison of Models 5, 6, and 8 Using Gender-Merged Survivorship Probabilities

Variable	Model 5	Model 6	Model 8
FLTEAR	-4.071	-3.894	-3.786
FLTEAR2	0.154	0.190	0.205
RACE	-0.305	-0.197	-0.234
SERLEN	0.007	0.006	0.005
_SERLEN	-0.043	-0.031	-0.012
SERLEN2	0.000	0.000	-0.001
_SERLEN2	0.001	0.000	0.000
RAGER1	-0.056	0.081	-0.039
RAGER2	-0.429	-0.473	-0.221
RAGER3	0.774	1.113	3.262
_RAGER1	-0.534	-0.394	-0.234
_RAGER2	-0.291	-0.306	-0.525
RCOHORT1	1.874	1.056	0.949
RCOHORT2	1.493	0.965	0.876
_RCOHORT1	5.404	3.691	2.344
_RCOHORT2	3.556	2.345	1.046
EDU1	-0.126	-0.084	-0.171
EDU2	-0.201	-0.148	-0.240
EDU3	-0.088	-0.045	-0.268
EDU4	0.203	0.140	0.170
_EDU1	-0.107	-0.138	-0.606
_EDU2	0.332	0.266	0.375
_EDU3	0.047	0.058	0.040
_EDU4	0.051	0.020	0.506
Intercept	92.560	94.233	95.34
R^2	0.849	0.848	0.611

ponents. The relationship between percentage of redistribution and lifetime earnings is, however, nonlinear (the coefficient β_1 is negative and β_2 is positive). Thus, the percentage of redistribution decreases at a decreasing rate as lifetime earnings increase. (Technically, the percentage of redistribution will at first decrease but later increase as lifetime earnings increase; however, given the range of LTEAR and FLTEAR in this study, the measured relationship between the percentage of redistribution and

Table 7.16. Married Regression Results: Comparison of Models 5, 6, and 8 Using Socioeconomic-Adjusted Survivorship Probabilities

Variable	Model 5	Model 6	Model 8
FLTEAR	-4.002	-3.791	-3.689
FLTEAR2	0.157	0.190	0.206
RACE	0.977	1.097	1.059
SERLEN	0.008	0.007	0.005
_SERLEN	-0.042	-0.030	-0.010
SERLEN2	0.000	0.000	-0.001
_SERLEN2	0.001	0.001	0.000
RAGER1	-0.044	0.117	0.007
RAGER2	-0.528	-0.565	-0.299
RAGER3	0.849	1.167	3.240
_RAGER1	-0.546	-0.435	-0.270
_RAGER2	-0.295	-0.297	-0.505
RCOHORT1	1.788	0.929	0.844
RCOHORT2	1.444	0.891	0.817
_RCOHORT1	5.359	3.711	2.401
_RCOHORT2	3.536	2.357	1.098
EDU1	-0.301	-0.270	-0.355
EDU2	0.084	0.151	0.050
EDU3	0.091	0.159	-0.066
EDU4	0.969	1.054	0.998
_EDU1	-0.038	-0.071	-0.529
_EDU2	0.309	0.239	0.345
_EDU3	0.055	0.064	0.060
_EDU4	0.055	0.009	0.469
Intercept	92.520	94.167	95.230
R^2	0.846	0.845	0.612

lifetime earnings was negative.) These results indicate that the OAI program (in 1972) clearly redistributed more, in relative terms, to persons with lower taxable earnings.

The inclusion of disaggregated survivorship probabilities did not reverse the inverse relationship between the redistribution measure and lifetime earnings. For the single model, accounting for mortality differentials by sex and race generally weakened the relationship between the redistribution and earnings measures (e.g., model 1 estimated LTEAR coefficient decreased from −4.426 to −4.166). But, further disaggregation by marital status, income, and education tended to strengthen the relationship over comparable estimates using sex and race differentials and, in several cases, over the similar estimates for age-only mortality differentials (e.g., model 2 estimated LTEAR increased from −4.871 with age-only mortality tables to −4.884 with socioeconomic-adjusted mortality tables). On the other hand, for married households, the relationship between the redistribution measures and lifetime earnings was consistently weakened when sex-race and sex-race-marital status-income-education differentials were introduced.

Therefore, the results indicate that enhanced longevity associated with educational attainment and income does not reverse or substantially weaken the progressivity of the program. From our findings on married households, mortality rates disaggregated by sex and race challenge the program's progressivity slightly less than mortality rates disaggregated by sex, race, marital status, income, and education. Quite different results were found for single workers. The OAI program was actually substantially more progressive (larger estimated LTEAR coefficients) when socioeconomic-adjusted mortality rates were used to calculate the annuity payment than when age-sex-race rates were used.

Findings on the effect of benefit indexing on the relationship between the percentage of redistribution and lifetime earnings varies across household types. For single households, the inclusion of indexing in the annuity counterfactual slightly strengthens the negative relationship between the percentage of redistribution and lifetime earnings in the models excluding the earnings test. That is, independent of the degree of mortality rate disaggregation, the OAI program was found to be more progressive for single households after the inclusion of benefit indexing in the annuity counterfactual. For all the married models, there is a stronger negative relationship between the percentage of redistribution of lifetime earnings *without* indexing. Hence, in all of the married models, the OAI program was found to be less progressive when the annuity counterfactual includes benefit indexing.

The addition of the earnings test consistently weakened the relationship between the percentage of redistribution and lifetime earnings for married households, but it consistently strengthened the relationship for single households. These findings are suggestive of different employment decisions by single and married households after retirement. The strengthening of the relationship for single households seems to indicate that single persons with lower lifetime earnings were more inclined to work after retirement. After examining the data set, it was found that 25 single households were affected by the earnings test, of which 65 percent were women. A majority of the households affected by the earnings test had lifetime earnings measures below the sample average. The labor force attachment of women after retirement may reflect not only the sex distribution of the retirement population, but also that single women typically have less physically demanding occupations that characteristically permit greater staying power.

The opposite was true for the married population. Generally speaking, high-income, married persons tended to continue working after retirement. The employment pattern of the married households is consistent with studies on retirement patterns (Boskin, 1977; Pechman, Aaron, and Taussig, 1968). In 1966, only 1.6 million of the 17 million persons eligible for retirement benefits were affected by the retirement test. Fifty percent of the 1.6 million beneficiaries affected by the earnings test earned $2,700 or more in 1966.

In general, the OAI program was found to be progressive with respect to lifetime earnings across all model permutations. The strength of the negative association between household percentage of redistribution and household earnings varied by marital status. In particular, the program had stronger progressive features for single households relative to married households.[3] This finding is not too surprising in light of the extra benefits extended to wives of covered workers (independent of family income).

Service Length

For the single models, the coefficients on SERLEN and SERLEN2 are negative and positive, respectively; the coefficients for SERLEN are significantly different from zero at a 1-percent level, but the coefficient for SERLEN2 is statistically significant in models 2 and 4 only. The coefficient for SERLEN is remarkably stable across the models, whereas the estimated coefficient for SERLEN2 modestly increases when program features are added to the annuity counterfactuals. The estimated negative, nonlinear association between the percentage of redistribution and service length suggests that longer contribution periods significantly reduce the percentage of redistribution received in retirement, ceteris paribus. That is, the program redistributed more in relative terms to single workers with shorter periods of participation.

The comparable sex-coded estimates for married persons are mixed and statistically insignificant. Again, the estimated coefficients are remarkably stable across survivorship assumptions. However, the coefficients for the service length variables SERLEN and _SERLEN tend toward zero when additional program features were introduced into the annuity counterfactual.

Sex

The sex variable was included in the single model only. The significance of the sex variable is sensitive to the choice of survivorship table used in the annuity calculation. Without mortality differentials by sex, benefit indexing, and the earnings test, the coefficient for SEX is negative and statistically insignificant. However, with the inclusion of sex and race differentials in survivorship, the coefficient for SEX is positive and significantly different from zero at a 1-percent level. This is because the monthly annuity counterfactual for women is reduced, reflecting women's greater longevity. Further disaggregation of mortality differentials by marital status, income, and education increased the redistributional gains of single women over single men. A major factor here is the allowance for marital status differentials in longevity. Single persons of both sexes have shorter life expectancies than their married counterparts, but the differential is greater for males than for females. As a result of their longevity, women received significant redistributional gains from the OAI program, ceteris paribus.

Single women also received further redistributional gains when benefit indexing and survivorship differentials by sex were included in the annuity counterfactual. The addition of the earnings test did not appreciably affect the female-to-male difference in the percentage of redistribution after accounting for benefit indexing and mortality differentials. Overall, females received redistribution components approximately 5 percentage points larger than their male counterparts when indexing, post-retirement earnings adjustments, and mortality differentials by sex were reflected in the annuity counterfactual.

Race

In the case of single households, the coefficient for RACE is small and statistically insignificant, with the notable exception of models 2 and 4 when benefit indexing and mortality differentials by sex, race, marital status, income, and education were accounted for in the annuity counterfactual. The sign for the RACE coefficient is mixed and dependent on counterfactual characteristics. Under the assumptions of model 1, the coefficient for RACE is positive, suggesting that nonwhites received a redistribution component slightly larger than their white counterparts, ceteris paribus. The slight gains of nonwhites are probably symptomatic of earnings differentials by race prevalent in the labor market. Whites, on average, receive higher earnings relative to nonwhites, concentrating nonwhites at the lower end of the progressive benefit formula. Even with the adjustments for sex and race differentials in mortality, the nonwhite redistributional gain persisted. However, the coefficient became smaller in magnitude with the allowances for race and sex differentials. This is because the somewhat less favorable survival rates for nonwhites increased the annuity level, thus lowering the size of the redistribution component. When survivor probabilities are adjusted for other socioeconomic factors, the coefficient changes sign but is still statistically insignificant. Again, adjustments in these factors raise the annuity level, causing an additional decline in the redistribution component. These results are consistent with Okonkwo (1976).

The inclusion of benefit indexing in the annuity counterfactual and mortality differentials by race and sex results in estimated coefficients that are negative. Further disaggregation of mortality rates by marital status, income, and education results in estimated coefficients that are negative and statistically significant. Identical sign-switching results occur with the addition of the earnings test.

Looking at the married model 5, the coefficients for RACE are negative and not statistically significant at a 10-percent level except when mortality differentials are disaggregated by sex, race, marital status, income, and education. The negative relationship between race and household percentage of redistribution is strengthened when mortality differentials by sex and race are included; however, when mortality differentials by sex, race, marital status, income, and education are included, the estimated coefficient for race is positive and statistically significant at either a 1- or 10-percent level except in model 7.

The effect of benefit indexing and the earnings test features on the coefficient estimate is dependent on the survivorship assumption; using the gender-merged and sex-race survivorship probabilities, the race differential is weakened with indexing but strengthened with the earnings test; however, using the socioeconomic-adjusted probabilities, the race differential is strengthened with indexing but weakened with the earnings test.

The mixed and contradictory results across married models and across the married and single models are perplexing. One contributing factor for the erratic performance of the race variable is the weak representation of nonwhites in the data set. Nonwhites accounted for 6 percent of the single households and 2 percent of married households. Clearly, any generalizations based on the size and sign of the estimated coefficients for RACE are tenuous and should be generalized with caution.

Age at Retirement

Most of the evidence on the age of retirement suggests that single persons received the largest redistributional component by retiring at age 65, ceteris paribus. This finding is consistent with earlier mentioned criticisms of the actuarial adjustment formulas. Except for RAGER3 (retirement after age 71), the estimated coefficients were small in magnitude and not significantly different from zero. The results indicate that the actuarial adjustment for early (before age 65) and late (between ages 65 and 72) retirement are relatively fair.

The coefficient for RAGER1, the variable for retirement prior to age 65, using the gender-merged survivorship table is negative and not statistically significant across all versions of the generalized single model. The inclusion of disaggregated mortality differentials reduces the size of the negative redistribution differential for persons who retired earlier than age 65 and, in some cases, reverses the sign of the redistribution differential. The addition of the benefit indexing feature to the annuity counterfactuals generally reverses the sign of the coefficient for RAGER1, whereas the earnings test feature does not significantly affect the size or sign of the coefficient.

The coefficient for RAGER2 (retirement between ages 65 and 72) is negative and statistically insignificant for all permutations of the generalized single model. The strength of the negative relationship decreases as mortality differentials are disaggregated. Similarly, benefit indexing and earnings test provisions further weaken the difference between the redistribution differential for persons retiring between ages 65 and 72 relative to persons retiring at age 65, ceteris paribus. The consistently negative sign on the RAGER2 dummy supports the expectation that benefit increments for late retirement (after age 65 and before age 72) are modestly inadequate.

The last retirement age variable to be discussed is RAGER3 (retirement after age 71). The coefficient for RAGER3 is negative and significantly different from zero at a 1- or 5-percent level for all single models. The size of the redistributional differential is augmented by mortality rate disaggregation, benefit indexing, and earnings test adjustments, with the notable exception of model 4 using mortality differentials by sex and race. This result suggests that benefit adjustments for persons retiring after age 72 are wholly inadequate. Changes in the law since 1972 have increased benefit increments for delayed retirement, so this feature of the law should affect current and future retirees somewhat differently.

Next, looking at the sex-coded retirement age variables for the married model, the results for RAGER1 are mixed and statistically insignificant. Early retirement for women does not significantly affect the size of the household redistribution measure relative to households in which the woman retired at age 65, ceteris paribus. However, the household redistribution measure is slightly smaller when the woman retired between the ages of 65 and 72 relative to age 65, ceteris paribus. The size of loss is slightly increased with increased disaggregation of mortality rates and the introduction of benefit indexing, but it is slightly reduced with the earnings test. The last retirement age variable is RAGER3. The coefficient for RAGER3 is positive and significantly different from zero at a 1-percent level for all models. In models 7 and 8, the redistribution component is over 3 percentage points larger if the female retired after age 72. The strength of this positive relationship is generally augmented by mortality rate disaggregation, benefit indexing, and earnings test adjustments. It is not surprising that women who postponed retirement to age 72 or later received abnormally high household redistribution measures. These women were most probably collecting special age-72 benefits, which are provided to aged persons who cannot claim benefits as a primary worker or dependent spouse and who have very few quarters of coverage; hence, OAI benefits were received by these women at a near-zero cost.

For married males, the coefficients for _RAGER1 and _RAGER2 in model 5 are negative and significantly different from zero at a 1-percent level. That is, the redistribution component is highest for married men who retire at age 65. Reduction in the redistribution component is greater for early retirement (ages 62–64) than for late retirement (ages 66–71). All males in the married data set retired before age 72. The strength of the relationship between redistribution and _RAGER2 is weakened by mortality disaggregation by sex and race but largely unaffected by further socioeconomic disaggregation. The opposite results are found for RAGER2 and the redistribution component. The household redistribution differential for males who retired after (before) age 65 increased (decreased) in magnitude with the inclusion of benefit indexing and earnings test adjustments in the annuity counterfactual.

Retirement Cohort

Estimates of the coefficients for RCOHORT1 (1962–1965) and RCOHORT2 (1966–1968) are positive and significantly different from zero at a 1-percent level for all permutations of the single and married generalized models. Also, the size of the coefficient for RCOHORT1 exceeds the size of the coefficient for RCOHORT2, suggesting that the gains from retiring in an earlier retirement cohort diminish over time.

For the single models, the effect of disaggregated mortality rates are mixed. When mortality differentials disaggregated by sex and race were used, the estimated coefficients for RCOHORT1 and RCOHORT2 diminish in size, reducing the intercohort redistributional differential. However, further disaggregation places upward pressure on the estimated size of the RCOHORT1 and RCOHORT2 coefficients; hence, the intercohort redistributional differential widens. It appears that the earlier cohorts had different educational and income characteristics, which tended to reverse the influence of sex and race differentials in survivorship on the redistribution measure. Other things equal, according to model 1, monthly benefits of persons retiring in the years 1962–1965 contained a redistribution share 8.975 to 9.634 percentage points higher than the monthly benefits of persons retiring after 1968. For persons retiring in the years 1966–1968, the difference ranges from 5.98 to 6.50 percentage points.

The addition of benefit indexing and the earnings test to the annuity counterfactual systematically narrows the intercohort redistributional differential, as expected. Since this study evaluates the OAI program in 1972 and retirement cohorts from 1962 to 1972 are included in the data set, benefit levels promised in real terms must be augmented over the retirement interval from 1962 to the year of program assessment, 1972. The benefit adjustment scheme indexed the initial annuity benefit in the retirement year by $(1 + c)^t$ where c is 0.0275 (the annuitized rate for future price changes) and t is the difference between the retirement year and 1972. Because of ex post indexing, the intercohort redistributional differential is narrowed. The narrowing effect of the earnings test feature was also expected, since the 1969–1972 retirement cohort had the greatest likelihood of receiving labor earnings in excess of the earnings limit in 1972, which would place upward pressure on the size of later cohorts' redistribution components, subsequently narrowing the redistributional differential across cohorts.

For the married models, similar results are obtained for the female-coded RCOHORT1 and RCOHORT2 coefficients. That is, disaggregated mortality differentials (sex-race *and* socioeconomic), benefit indexing, and the earnings test adjustments tended to narrow the intercohort redistributional differential. However, the male-coded _RCOHORT1 and _RCOHORT2 coefficients are invariant to the level of mortality rate disaggregation, but they tended to diminish in size with the addition of benefit indexing and the earnings test, ceteris paribus.

Level of Education

With the exception of the coefficient for EDU4, the estimated coefficients for the education variables in the single models are generally negative and statistically insignificant. That is, the redistributional differential by education level is negative, albeit small, for households with less than eight years of education or high school training relative to households with eighth-grade education only. The influence of different mortality rate assumptions is mixed. For households with less than eight years of education or more than 12 years of education, the inclusion of sex and race differentials in survivorship tended to either eliminate existing redistributional gains or increase redistributional losses relative to households with eighth-grade educations.

However, further disaggregation of mortality rates by marital status, income, and education generally reduced the redistributional gap between households with eight years of education and those with 12 or more years of education but expanded the gap between households with eight years of education and those with less than eight years. This result is reflective of the inverse relationship between mortality and education and income levels. Mortality disaggregation tended to diminish the negative differential between households with nine to 11 years of education and those with eight years of education. Furthermore, benefit indexing narrowed the education redistributional differential. But the earnings test tended to widen the differential for households with less than eight and 12 years of education, while it generally narrowed the differential for households with nine to 11 and 13 or more years of education. The earnings test effect suggests that persons with nine to 11 or 13 or more years of education tended to remain in the labor force after retirement.

Again, the coefficient estimates for the sex-coded education variables in the married models are mixed and generally statistically insignificant. However, a few patterns are worth mentioning. For all education groupings except EDU4, the inclusion of sex and race differentials in survivorship tended to narrow the education redistributional differentials, whereas further disaggregation tended to improve the redistribution status of households with any of the following education variables: EDU2, EDU3, EDU4, _EDU1, _EDU3, and _EDU4. The inclusion of the earnings test greatly increased the positive redistribution differential for males with college education, while it increased the negative redistributional differential for households with any of the following education variables: EDU1, EDU2, EDU3, and _EDU1. Again, these results are reflective of postretirement employment patterns of married households.

8

Assessing the Success of the Old-Age Insurance Program in Redistributing Income

The study described in chapters 3 through 7 examined the extent to which the old-age insurance portion of the Social Security program redistributed income among subgroups comprising the same retirement population. Subgroups were distinguished by socioeconomic traits, such as sex, race, marital status, income, and education. In estimating the distributional impact of the Social Security program, the study stressed the importance of an intertemporal framework to evaluate a lifetime public program and the need to account for demographic factors, such as differential mortality rates. An actuarial standard of fairness was employed to measure intra- and intergenerational redistribution.

This chapter assesses the distributional performance of the 1972 OAI program. The first section presents answers to the five interrelated issues raised in the introduction and study conclusions. The chapter concludes with policy recommendations for improving the program's future performance.

Summary of Study Findings

Progressivity Assessment

This study offers further evidence of the redistributive nature of Social Security. The tabular and regression results presented in chapters 5 and 7, respectively, provide additional confirmation of the generally progressive effect of the 1972 OAI benefit formula.[1] Tabular results showed that the percentage of redistribution ranged from 97.6 percent for families with incomes less than $1,000 to 89.3 percent for families with incomes in excess of $20,000. Recall that the estimated relationship between the percentage of redistribution and lifetime earnings was negative and nonlinear. Overall, the program was generally more effective in redistributing income when the annuity payment did not account for the earnings test, price indexing, and disaggregated survivorship probabilities.

Contrary to Aaron's study (1977), socioeconomic differentials in survivorship do not reverse the direction of redistribution. Both the tabular and regression results indicate that the longer life expectancies among the more affluent only slightly dampen the programs' progressivity. In fact, the regression results show that mortality rates disaggregated by sex and race challenge the program's progressivity slightly less than the highly disaggregated socioeconomic mortality rates.

In conclusion, this study of the 1972 retirement cohort showed that 1) all income groups received more than their money's worth from the OAI program, and 2) the benefit formula favors workers with low earnings. These conclusions hold independent of the program features and survivorship probabilities built into the annuity counterfactual.

The Effect of Sex Differentials in Survivorship on Program Performance

The distributional impact of the OAI program was found to be sensitive to the tailoring of annuity benefits to reflect sex differentials in survivorship. Generally speaking, single females and married couples were made differentially better off and single males were made worse off in a sex-neutral retirement system relative to a sex discriminating, actuarially fair retirement system. Single female beneficiaries as a group received annuity benefits that were approximately 16 percent larger in a sex-neutral retirement system relative to a sex-race discriminating system, whereas their male counterparts as a group received benefits that were approximately 7 percent smaller. Furthermore, when the mortality rates were disaggregated by sex, race, marital status, income, and education, single female beneficiaries received annuity benefits that were approximately 9 percent larger in a sex-neutral retirement system, whereas single male beneficiaries received benefits that were approximately 23 percent smaller.

Similar comparisons were not as useful among married beneficiaries because the joint-and-two-thirds annuity covered the lives of the husband and wife; hence, any sex differentials were largely offset by dual insurance coverage. Nonetheless, actuarially fair benefits for married persons were approximately 3 percent higher, independent of the sex of the primary annuitant, in a sex-neutral retirement system relative to a sex discriminating system. The sex-neutral bias in favor of married persons as a group is a result of the joint-and-two-thirds annuity, which insures the life of the shorter-lived male, the longer-lived female, and the longest-lived survivor, who is typically female. The sex-neutral bias increased when the socioeconomic discriminating system was used as the comparison system.

The estimated coefficient for SEX in the single generalized model was positive and statistically significant, supporting the tabular findings. All other things equal, single female beneficiaries received redistribution components approximately 3 percentage points larger than their male counterparts when survivorship probabilities were disaggregated by sex and race. The marginal gain increased to 5.2 percentage points when survivorship probabilities were further disaggregated by marital status, income, and education (model 4 results).

The Effect of the Wife's Work Status on Program Performance

The influence of the wife's work status was examined extensively in chapter 5. To address this issue, households in which both members were retired in 1972 were divided into one-earner and two-earner units. A two-earner household was defined as a household where both members qualified for primary-worker benefits. Alternatively, a one-earner household meant only the male member qualified for primary-worker benefits and the spouse was not collecting worker benefits. Independent of sex and family type, all individuals received positive income transfers from the OAI program in 1972. Overall, the traditional family structure received preferential treatment from the OAI program because the nonworking wife received retirement benefits without payment of extra contributions. On average, one-earner households received 3.3 percentage points more redistribution per dollar of OAI benefits than their two-earner couple counterparts.

First, the effect of the wife's work status on wife-only benefit incidence was small. In absolute terms, working women paid in more dollars in the form of OAI contributions, and, in exchange, they received higher OAI benefit levels. However, the difference in percentage of redistribution per dollar of OAI benefits for working and nonworking women was extremely small, suggesting that women, independent of work status, were treated almost equally in terms of redistribution.

The finding of roughly equal treatment among women who made different labor-homemaker choices did not apply to men married to women who made different labor-homemaker choices. Generally speaking, the percentage of redistribution was generally higher for males in one-earner households relative to their male counterparts in two-earner households. The apparent redistributional differential was symptomatic of the very low annuity benefits received from the nonworking wife's joint-and-two-thirds annuity.

In conclusion, although women with different work statuses paid in different amounts of OAI contributions, they were treated roughly equally in terms of the percentage of OAI benefits representing redistribution. The redistribution pattern for males by household type was similar; however, the absolute size of the percentage of redistribution was larger for males in one-earner households across all income categories. While women were treated roughly equally, working women received a significantly smaller percentage of redistribution when comparisons were made with working males. The working woman received the smallest return on her OAI contributions relative to her male counterpart because of her retirement and employment characteristics and the community property assumption underpinning the annuity-type counterfactual. Lastly, the OAI program was found to be more progressive and less regressive across income categories for two-earner relative to one-earner households as reflected by the high-income-group-comparison approach to progressivity assessment.

The Effect of Marital Status on Program Performance

The OAI program was clearly tilted against the interests of single men. Single men are less favorably treated because they are forced to participate in a retirement program that taxes the individual but pays benefits on the basis of the family unit. This program bias is compounded by the single male's shorter life expectancy. Single women fare better in a family-based retirement program relative to single men because of their longer life expectancies. While single women fare better than their single male counterparts, they do not receive redistribution components comparable to married men because of the difference in insurance coverage purchased on the date of retirement (individual versus joint-and-two-thirds annuity).

The Distribution of Spousal Benefits

The OAI program was found to allocate redistribution components proportionately across quintile groups, independent of family type and sex. Contrary to the 1937–1939 Advisory Council's intent, dependents benefits were, at best, proportionally distributed to dependent spouses of male workers. Evidence from this life-cycle study supports the earlier findings of Holden (1979 and 1982). It demonstrated that supplemental benefits may not be adequately serving the 1939 objective of protecting a group of aged persons experiencing economic hardship. This suggests, perhaps, that a more effective target definition should be used to determine need aside from the work status of the female, which is currently used by Social Security.

Conclusions

Overall, all 1972 beneficiaries received more than their money's worth from the OAI program. In addition, the OAI program was found to be mildly and generally progressive across income groups, but it also exhibited regressive features, resulting in lower relative returns to middle-income beneficiaries. The regressive features were more pronounced with the introduction of the earnings test and socioeconomic-adjusted mortality rates. Lower-income groups received the largest relative gains from the program, whereas the middle-income groups received the largest share of the intergenerational transfer. The size of the redistribution transfer was found, in many cases, to be significantly associated with the following worker characteristics: lifetime earnings, service length, sex, retirement age, year of retirement, and marital status.

The results presented in chapters 5 and 7 offer a snapshot of the OAI program for a single year, 1972. Since 1972, however, Social Security legislation has changed modestly with the enactment of the 1983 Social Security Amendments. The 1983 amendments were designed to solve the short-term and long-term financial problems of the system, not program inequities. Congress in 1983 took a three-prong approach to rescuing Social Security from financial insolvency: 1) increasing revenue (expanding covered occupations, taxing Social Security benefits, and raising taxes); 2) decreasing benefits (delaying cost-of-living adjustments and reducing early retirement benefits); and 3) reducing the retirement rate (raising the retirement age and raising the delayed retirement credit). Legislation enacted in 1983 did very little to correct the inequities in the system, especially those inequities stemming from the provision of noncontributory spousal benefits.[2] Future amendments are needed to solve the equity problems mentioned in this book.

Policy Recommendations

From a policy point of view, this study has several noteworthy implications. First, evidence showed that the OAI program, as legislated in 1972, was not distributionally neutral, and its distributional impact often depended on factors incidental to the program (e.g., differences in longevity). Second, the legislated preferential treatment of women, traditional family structures, and earlier retirement cohorts draws into question and challenges the redistribution objective of the OAI program. Third, it was found that the intended and actual effects of statutory provisions (actuarial reduction for early retirement, delayed retirement credit, earnings test, and benefit indexing) may vary widely and may, as a result, jeopardize the overall effectiveness of the program.

The need to reform Social Security has been recognized by nearly every government commission studying the program in the last two decades. The well-documented long-term changes in demographic, economic, and social trends affecting American families have strained the terms of the social contract between the generations embodied in Social Security. If the system is to meet the current and future retirement needs of Americans, then reform is in order today. The reform recommendations proposed in this section speak to the inequities between single and married persons, one-earner and two-earner couples, and earlier and later cohorts. These inequities can be eliminated by adopting two types of reform: family and intercohort. Family reform involves the modernization of the system's treatment of the family. In essence, the traditional 1939 family paradigm underlying the current system would be replaced with a family paradigm more reflective of contemporary society. Intercohort reform, on the other hand, necessitates a reexamination of the social compact between the generations. Policymakers would be required to adopt a principle of intergenerational equity that defines the benefit rights and financial obligations of all retirement cohorts. Specific reform recommendations for each reform type are presented in this section.

Intercohort Reform

The unequal treatment of later cohorts is likely to lead to intergenerational conflict, which may, in time, threaten the future viability and, perhaps, existence of the program. As long as Social Security benefits are financed by a "pay as you go" financing scheme, instead of by actual contributions made by workers, the system will be sensitive to unpredictable changes in demographic, economic, and political conditions. Also, the deficit financing scheme permits disjointed benefit level and contribution rate decisions. That is, it allows a generous society (or administration) to liberalize retirement benefits and pass the bill to future generations retrospectively. Retrospective debt assignment can encourage financial irresponsibility on behalf of myopic policymakers and adds a stochastic element to the tax liability of current taxpayers, complicating their life-cycle decision-making process.

The days of financial irresponsibility and indiscriminate cost shifting are rapidly drawing to a close. Today's taxpayers are asked to pay for the retirement benefits of an ever-growing number of retirees. At the same time, Congress, at least in the recent past, has liberalized benefit levels, adding to the Social Security debt load of current taxpayers. In return for the intergenerational transfers, current taxpayers (future retirees) are promised an ever-shrinking return on their OAI tax contributions. This is hardly a stable social compact between the generations. Intergenerational conflict could be avoided if policymakers established a principle of intergenerational equity that clearly specifies the retired population's benefit rights and the working population's financial obligation to the retired population.

To insure a stable social compact between generations, a principle of intergenerational equity must establish: 1) a specific criteria defining benefit rights for each retired cohort, 2) a specific criteria defining Social Security debt obligations for each taxpaying cohort, 3) a connection between the expenditure and revenue sides of the retirement system, and 4) a measure of equity for comparative analysis of intergenerational treatment. Policymakers could use this principle to make assurances to each retirement cohort that retirement benefit levels and contribution tax rates are reasonable, adequate, and fair and to assess the program's treatment of each cohort participating in the program.

My recommendation for a principle of intergenerational equity is fashioned on the actuarially fair insurance conditions described in chapter 3.[3] Recall that the intergenerational condition for an actuarially fair insurance program was:

$$\sum_{i=1}^{n} TC_i = \sum_{i=1}^{n} B_i^{s,c}. \qquad (8.1)$$

That is, each retirement cohort receives retirement benefits equal to the present value of its OAI tax contributions.[4] All four aspects of the intergenerational equity principle definition are satisfied by condition 8.1. Each retired population would be assured aggregate benefits equal to its past OAI contributions plus interest. The taxpayer population has a defined Social Security debt load equal to the current retired population's past OAI contributions plus interest. But, in exchange for the intergenerational loan, the taxpayer population is guaranteed a future benefit stream equal to its OAI contributions plus interest. A stable social compact between the generations is implemented. Also, the equality between benefit and tax streams in condition 8.1 draws together the expenditure and revenue sides of the program. Intergenerational equity comparisons are easily implemented by estimating condition 8.1.

Note that this definition of intergenerational equity ties benefit streams to OAI contributions and also relies on a deficit funding scheme. Figure

8.1 illustrates the financing scheme underlying my recommendation. Each cohort receives a benefit steam, in present value terms, equal to its past OAI contributions plus interest, and they know, ex ante, their debt obligation to the current retirement population. This simple system is straightforward provided the mortality, fertility, and labor force participation experiences between the cohorts are identical. This is not likely the case. For instance, if retirement cohorts A and C were smaller in number than cohort B, then cohort B's debt obligation may be relatively low. But to guarantee adequate retirement benefits in retirement, cohort B may require a larger benefit stream in retirement (hence, it may need to save more for the future). Two options are possible. One, cohort B could generate a contribution surplus (contributions in excess of retirement cohort A's OAI contributions plus interest), which would be accumulated for the cohort in a trust fund to be repaid during retirement. Thus, retirement cohort C would have a debt obligation equal to retirement cohort B's OAI tax contribution plus interest *minus* the accumulated surplus. Alternatively, cohort B could incur a Social Security debt load equal to cohort A's past OAI contributions plus interest and accept a lower retirement benefit when it retires. An adequacy bound to benefit levels may be necessary to ensure a reasonable level of income security at retirement.

The actuarial principle of intergenerational equity has many advantages. First, it integrates the expenditure and revenue sides of the lifetime retirement program. That is, it makes explicit who is paying for what the program is providing. Second, the taxpayer population's debt obligation is known ex ante. They owe the current retired population a benefit stream equivalent to its past OAI contributions compounded at a reasonable interest rate, thereby minimizing long-range planning distortions. Third, the cohort's future retirement benefit stream is also known in advance. Hence, young cohorts can form reasonable expectations on the retirement sup-

Figure 8.1. Three Generation Example of the Actuarially Fair Principle of Intergenerational Equity

	Retirement		Employment
Retirement Cohort A	Benefits	=	Contributions + interest
Retirement Cohort B	Benefits	=	Contributions + interest
Retirement Cohort C	Benefits	=	Contributions + interest

port received from Social Security in the future and then supplement the expected support with private pensions and savings. Fourth, the proposed principle promotes intergenerational consensus, not conflict, since each cohort has consistently defined benefit rights and debt obligations.

Intergenerational conflict and tension can be eliminated and intergenerational disaster avoided if policymakers are ready to make fiscally responsible and fair intergenerational decisions. The proposed principle of intergenerational equity would guarantee both fairness and financial responsibility. But it requires structural change within the system, not mere fine tuning or disjointed incrementalism. It is unlikely, however, that major structural change to eliminate intercohort inequities is forthcoming any time soon.

Family Reform

Social Security embodies a particular perception of the family and of government responsibility to protect the family unit. Since its inception, the program has protected the traditional family consisting of a breadwinner husband and a dependent wife who remains at home to care for children. Relatively few American families conform to the traditional family pattern. Changes over the last 30 years in long-term patterns of fertility and female labor participation strongly challenge the government's perception of the family. Commensurate structural changes in the program's design are necessary if the Social Security program is going to meet the needs of today's nontraditional American society.

My family reform recommendation requires both modernizing the family paradigm and redefining the benefit base underpinning the Social Security system. The current system rests on a 1939 family paradigm that produces benefit-tax base inconsistencies. The 1939 provision of (noncontributory) dependent spouse benefits resulted in a system that taxes the individual worker but assigns benefits on the basis of the family unit. Consequently, one-earner couples are more favorably treated than single workers and two-earner couples. I propose adopting the earnings sharing reform proposal to eliminate these inequities because it embodies an interdependent-economic partnership concept of marriage and an individual base unit for taxing and paying benefits.[5] Although the earnings sharing proposal implies the elimination of spousal and survivor benefits, homemaker protection and individual life style choice are assured without appealing to an outdated family paradigm.

Earnings sharing is based on the philosophy that marriage is an economic partnership and that assets (including earnings credits) accumulated during marriage should be divided equally between spouses, independent of each spouse's time allocation between paid and unpaid employment.[6] That is, a community property principle is invoked in assigning within household ownership rights to family-owned assets, thereby making earnings credits portable in the event of divorce or death. In the case of Social Security earnings credits, the earnings of the husband and wife would be split equally for the purpose of computing individual retirement benefits. Earnings are shared for the duration of the marriage. A single person's Social Security benefits would be based on her(his) individually earned credits. A married person's Social Security benefits would be based on any credits the individual earned before and after marriage, plus half the couple's total earnings in each year of marriage. The surviving spouse would inherit the credits if the husband or wife dies. Therefore, each individual, independent of marital status and spouse's employment status, would receive retirement benefits on her (his) own right.

The earnings sharing reform would eliminate the inequities between single and married persons, one-earner and two-earner couples, and divorced persons married less than 10 years and all other divorced persons. In addition, earnings sharing would establish an individually based benefit base and adopt a modern family paradigm that would be neutral with regard to male and female labor force participation decisions within the family. This family reform proposal has strong intuitive appeal because it is based on the principle of equality.

The earnings sharing proposal is not without its problems. The Social Security Administration recently completed an internal evaluation of a wide range of such proposals.[7] The study concluded that the reform proposals under consideration would reduce many people's benefits (especially men married to women who choose not to work outside the home), would be expensive to implement, and would not easily mesh with the current system unless there was a long phase-in period. But while there are bound to be net losers in the transition between the two systems, there are a large number who would gain now and in the future by modernizing the system.

After intercohort and family reform proposals are implemented, policymakers need to address the issue of intracohort redistribution. How much intracohort redistribution from the lifetime rich to the lifetime poor is deemed socially desirable? Does the current redistributive benefit formula achieve the desirable redistribution? In answering these important questions, policymakers would be well-advised to control for the effect of socioeconomic status on longevity to insure that the program's performance is consistent with its legislated intent.

For the most part, the inequities between single and married persons, one-earner and two-earner couples, women divorced after 10 years of marriage and all other divorced women, and earlier and later cohorts could be eliminated if policymakers adopt an actuarially fair principle of intergenerational equity and the earnings sharing family reform proposal. The transition from the current system to the new system will require major structural changes and will, most likely, erode the financial status of some groups of beneficiaries. Nonetheless, to insure Social Security's responsiveness and fairness to the current and future generations of Americans, reforms promoting more equitable treatment of single persons, married working women, divorced women, and later retirement cohorts must be given top priority now, before it is too late.

Appendix 1

Data Set Descriptions

The data set used in this study is a subsample of the 1973 Exact Match File, a nationally representative sample of all Americans in 1972. A respondent in the Match File was included in the subsample if she or he was a "good match," 62 or older in 1972, and received Social Security benefits in 1972. Two data sets were constructed: single and married.

The single data set included 353 respondents: 138 males (39 percent of all single respondents) and 215 females (61 percent of all single respondents). There were 2,771 couples included in the married data set in which at least one member of the couple satisfied the sorting criteria. The total number of respondents included in the study was 5,895. The following tables describe the characteristics of the data sets.

Table A1.1. Summary Statistics

Total population	5,895	
Marital status		
Married	5,542	(94% of sample)
Single	353	(6% of sample)
Race		
White	5,643	(96% of sample)
Nonwhite	252	(4% of sample)
Men		
Total	2,909	(49% of sample)
Marital status		
Married	2,771	(95%)
Single	138	(5%)
Median age		
Married		
White	69	
Nonwhite	69	
Single		
White	69	
Nonwhite	69	
Women		
Total	2,986	(51% of sample)
Marital status		
Married	2,771	(93%)
Single	215	(7%)
Median age		
Married		
White	66	
Nonwhite	61	
Single		
White	70	
Nonwhite	69	

Table A1.2. Age Distribution by Race, Marital Status, and Sex

Race, marital status, and sex	Age in 1972					
	Less than 61	62-64	65	66-72	More than 72	Total
White						
Married						
Men	50	282	197	1,344	783	2,656
Women	610	512	174	1,035	325	2,656
Nonmarried						
Men	0	18	13	64	33	128
Women	0	13	12	125	53	203
Nonwhite						
Married						
Men	1	15	8	60	31	115
Women	60	12	4	32	7	115
Nonmarried						
Men	0	2	0	7	1	10
Women	0	5	0	4	3	12
	721	859	408	2,671	1,236	5,985

Table A1.3. Retirement Year Distribution by Marital Status, Sex, and Age

Marital status, sex, and age		Year of retirement												
		1962	1963	1964	1965	1966	1967	1968	1969	1970	1971	1972	1973+	Total
Nonmarried men														
62-64		0	0	0	0	0	0	0	0	3	11	6	0	20
65		0	0	0	0	0	0	2	5	1	3	2	0	13
66-72		1	1	10	7	7	14	7	9	7	4	4	0	71
73 and over		8	7	4	5	4	1	3	1	0	0	1	0	34
		9	8	14	12	11	15	12	15	11	18	13	0	138
Nonmarried women														
62-64		0	0	0	0	0	0	0	0	6	7	5	0	18
65		0	0	0	0	0	0	0	2	3	3	4	0	12
66-72		5	8	7	9	19	15	24	13	14	10	5	0	129
73 and over		21	4	6	9	10	3	2	0	0	1	0	0	56
		26	12	13	18	29	18	26	15	23	21	14	0	215
Married men														
61 <	0	0	0	0	0	0	0	0	0	0	0	0	51	51
62-64	0	0	0	0	0	0	0	0	0	68	88	113	28	297
65	0	0	0	0	0	0	0	0	79	26	25	74	1	205
66-72	0	30	46	82	124	179	187	235	181	139	126	66	9	1,404
73 and over	210	204	116	82	54	42	34	30	15	9	8	1	9	814
	210	234	162	164	178	221	221	265	275	242	247	254	98	2,771
Married women														
61 <	0	0	0	0	0	0	0	0	0	0	0	0	670	670
62-64	0	0	0	0	0	0	0	0	0	119	161	159	85	524
65	0	0	0	0	0	0	0	0	112	32	14	18	2	178
66-72	0	54	74	110	131	158	158	175	85	57	34	15	16	1,067
73 and over	120	69	49	26	20	17	2	6	7	4	5	1	6	332
	120	123	123	136	151	175	160	181	204	212	214	193	719	2,771

Table A1.4. Distribution by Years of School Completed and Family Income in 1972: Men Only

Years of school completed	Family income in 1972							
	Married men				Nonmarried men			
	$0-4,000	$4,001-6,000	$6,001-10,000	$10,001+	$0-4,000	$4,001-6,000	$6,001-10,000	$10,001+
Total number	724	697	711	639	77	17	18	26
Total percent	26	25	26	23	56	12	13	19
Elementary								
Less than 8 years	313	182	140	74	33	1	4	6
8 years	211	215	200	134	21	9	6	6
High school								
1-3 years	94	137	124	105	11	2	0	1
4 years	63	106	149	155	7	4	3	7
College								
1-3 years	25	31	45	59	2	1	3	1
4 or more	18	26	53	112	3	0	2	5

Table A1.5. Distribution by Years of School Completed and Family Income in 1972: Women Only

Years of school completed	Family income in 1972							
	Married women				Nonmarried women			
	$0-4,000	$4,001-6,000	$6,001-10,000	$10,001+	$0-4,000	$4,001-6,000	$6,001-10,000	$10,001+
Total number	724	697	711	639	100	41	38	36
Total percent	26	25	26	23	46	19	18	17
Elementary								
Less than 8 years	241	154	85	40	21	3	4	3
8 years	202	177	144	98	14	7	4	2
High school								
1-3 years	127	118	149	108	11	2	6	4
4 years	120	174	230	214	36	20	15	11
College								
1-3 years	23	54	61	86	4	3	3	4
4 or more	11	20	42	93	14	6	6	12

Table A1.6. Distribution of Claim Status by Sex, Marital Status, and Age

Sex, marital status, and age	Claim status		
	Primary-worker	Dependent spouse	Not collecting
Men			
Married			
61 <	0	0	51
62-64	268	0	29
65	204	0	1
66-72	1,389	2	13
73+	803	0	11
Nonmarried			
62-64	20	0	0
65	13	0	0
66-72	71	0	0
73+	34	0	0
Women			
Married			
61 <	0	0	670
62-64	234	218	72
65	96	80	2
66-72	521	531	15
73+	147	179	6
Nonmarried			
62-64	18	0	0
65	12	0	0
66-72	129	0	0
73+	56	0	0
Total	4,015	1,010	870

Appendix 2

Additional Descriptive Results

Table A2.1. Changes in the Percentage of Redistribution Due to Indexing for Married, Both-Retired Households

Total family income in 1972	Gender-merged, earnings-adjusted			Sex-race-distinct, earnings-adjusted		
	Type-1 (1) Nonindexed[a]	Type-4 (2) Indexed[a]	(2)-(1) Change in percentage of redistribution	Type-2 (3) Nonindexed[a]	Type-5 (4) Indexed[a]	(4)-(3) Change in percentage of redistribution
0- 1,000	97.4	97.7	0.3	97.5	97.8	0.3
1,001- 1,500	93.1	93.9	0.8	93.3	94.1	0.8
1,501- 2,000	90.7	91.8	1.1	90.9	92.0	1.1
2,001- 2,500	90.4	91.3	0.9	90.5	91.6	1.1
2,501- 3,000	89.6	90.6	1.0	89.7	91.0	1.3
3,001- 3,500	88.2	89.4	1.2	88.4	89.7	1.3
3,501- 4,000	87.4	88.6	1.2	87.6	88.9	1.3
4,001- 5,000	86.8	88.2	1.4	87.1	88.6	1.5
5,001- 6,000	86.0	87.5	1.5	86.3	87.9	1.6
6,001- 8,000	85.4	87.1	1.7	85.7	87.5	1.8
8,001-10,000	85.9	87.7	1.8	86.2	88.1	1.9
10,001-20,000	87.4	88.9	1.5	87.6	89.3	1.7
20,001+	87.1	88.6	1.5	87.3	88.9	1.6

[a]Raw data used to calculate the percentage of redistribution for each family income classification are available upon request.

Table A2.2. Changes in the Percentage of Redistribution under Different Survivorship Probability Assumptions, Nonearning-Test-Adjusted for Married, Both-Retired Households

Total family income in 1972	Annuity-type, indexed			Change in percentage of redistribution	
	Type-1[a] (4)	Type-2[a] (5)	Type-3[a] (6)	(5)-(4)	(6)-(4)
0- 1,000	97.7	97.8	97.6	0.1	-0.1
1,001- 1,500	93.9	94.1	92.9	0.2	-1.0
1,501- 2,000	91.8	92.0	91.3	0.2	-0.5
2,001- 2,500	91.1	91.4	91.1	0.3	0.0
2,501- 3,000	90.3	90.6	90.3	0.3	0.0
3,001- 3,500	89.1	89.5	89.1	0.4	0.0
3,501- 4,000	88.3	88.6	88.4	0.3	0.1
4,001- 5,000	87.9	88.3	88.2	0.4	0.3
5,001- 6,000	87.1	87.6	87.5	0.5	0.4
6,001- 8,000	86.4	86.8	86.8	0.4	0.4
8,001-10,000	86.6	87.1	87.1	0.5	0.5
10,001-20,000	87.1	87.5	87.6	0.4	0.5
20,001+	87.0	87.4	87.7	0.4	0.7
Mean	87.6	88.0	88.0	0.4	0.4

[a]Raw data used to calculate the percentage of redistribution for each family income classification are available upon request.

Table A2.3. Summary Percentage Point Comparisons for Married, Both-Retired Households by Annuity Type, Sex, and Household Type

	Type-1		Type-2		Type-3		Type-4		Type-5		Type-6	
	Two-earner	One-earner	Two-earner	One-earner	Two-earner	One-earner	Two-earner	One-earner	Two-earner	One-earner	Two-earner	One-earner
Poorest to richest percentage point gap												
Female	6	7	6	6	6	6	6	6	5	7	4	6
Male	7	3	6	3	6	3	6	3	6	4	5	3
Household unit	7	4	6	4	6	4	6	4	6	4	5	4
Highest percentage of redistribution												
Female	87	90	88	90	88	90	89	91	89	92	89	92
Male	93	96	93	96	93	96	94	96	94	97	94	97
Household unit	91	94	91	94	91	94	92	95	92	95	92	95
Lowest percentage of redistribution												
Female	78	79	79	79	79	79	81	81	81	81	81	81
Male	86	91	86	91	86	91	87	92	88	92	88	92
Household unit	83	87	83	87	84	88	85	88	85	89	86	89

Table A2.4. Male-to-Female Differences in Percentage of Redistribution Controlling for Family Income and Family Type

Total family income in 1972	Type-1			Type-2			Type-3		
	Female	Male	Difference	Female	Male	Difference	Female	Male	Difference
Two-earner									
0- 2,000	87	93	+6	88	93	+5	88	93	+5
2,001- 2,500	88	93	+5	88	93	+5	88	93	+5
2,501- 3,000	88	92	+4	88	92	+4	88	92	+4
3,001- 3,500	84	88	+4	85	88	+3	84	88	+4
3,501- 4,000	81	88	+7	82	89	+7	82	89	+7
4,001- 5,000	80	87	+7	80	87	+7	80	87	+7
5,001- 6,000	78	87	+9	79	87	+8	79	87	+8
6,001- 8,000	79	86	+7	80	86	+6	80	86	+6
8,001-10,000	80	86	+6	81	86	+5	81	86	+5
10,001-20,000	84	87	+3	84	87	+3	84	88	+4
20,001+	81	86	+5	82	87	+5	82	87	+5
One-earner									
0- 2,000	90	96	+6	90	96	+6	90	96	+6
2,001- 2,500	90	96	+6	90	96	+6	91	96	+5
2,501- 3,000	85	94	+9	86	94	+8	86	94	+8
3,001- 3,500	84	93	+9	85	93	+8	85	93	+8
3,501- 4,000	82	92	+10	82	92	+10	82	92	+10
4,001- 5,000	83	92	+9	83	93	+10	83	93	+10
5,001- 6,000	79	91	+12	79	91	+12	79	91	+12
6,001- 8,000	80	91	+11	81	91	+10	81	91	+10
8,001-10,000	79	91	+12	79	91	+12	79	91	+12
10,001-20,000	82	92	+10	82	92	+10	83	92	+9
20,001+	83	93	+10	84	93	+9	84	93	+9

Table A2.5. Family-Type Differences in Percentage of Redistribution Controlling for Family Income and Sex

Total family income in 1972	Type-1			Type-2			Type-3		
	Two-earner	One-earner	Dif-ference	Two-earner	One-earner	Dif-ference	Two-earner	One-earner	Dif-ference
Females									
0- 2,000	87	90	+3	88	90	+2	88	90	+2
2,001- 2,500	88	90	+2	88	90	+2	88	91	+3
2,501- 3,000	88	85	-3	88	86	-2	88	86	-2
3,001- 3,500	84	84	0	85	85	0	84	85	+1
3,501- 4,000	81	82	+1	82	82	0	82	82	0
4,001- 5,000	80	83	+3	80	83	+3	80	83	+3
5,001- 6,000	78	79	+1	79	79	0	79	79	0
6,001- 8,000	79	80	+1	80	81	+1	80	81	+1
8,001-10,000	80	79	-1	81	79	-2	81	79	-2
10,001-20,000	84	82	-2	84	82	-2	84	83	-1
20,001+	81	83	+2	82	84	+2	82	84	+2
Males									
0- 2,000	93	96	+3	93	96	+3	93	96	+3
2,001- 2,500	93	96	+3	93	96	+3	93	96	+3
2,501- 3,000	92	94	+2	92	94	+2	92	94	+2
3,001- 3,500	88	93	+5	88	93	+5	88	93	+5
3,501- 4,000	88	92	+4	89	92	+3	89	92	+3
4,001- 5,000	87	92	+5	87	93	+6	87	93	+6
5,001- 6,000	87	91	+4	87	91	+4	87	91	+4
6,001- 8,000	86	91	+5	86	91	+5	86	91	+5
8,001-10,000	86	91	+5	86	91	+5	86	91	+5
10,001-20,000	87	92	+5	87	92	+5	88	92	+4
20,001+	86	93	+7	87	93	+6	87	93	+6

Table A2.6. Nonindexed-to-Indexed Differences in Percentage of Redistribution Controlling for Family Income and Household Unit

	Type-1			Type-2			Type-3		
	Non-indexed	Indexed	Dif-ference	Non-indexed	Indexed	Dif-ference	Non-indexed	Indexed	Dif-ference
Two-earner									
0- 2,000	91	92	+1	91	92	+1	91	92	+1
2,001- 2,500	91	92	+1	92	93	+1	92	93	+1
2,501- 3,000	90	91	+1	90	91	+1	90	91	+1
3,001- 3,500	87	88	+1	87	88	+1	87	88	+1
3,501- 4,000	86	87	+1	86	87	+1	86	87	+1
4,001- 5,000	84	86	+2	85	86	+1	85	86	+1
5,001- 6,000	84	85	+1	84	86	+2	84	86	+2
6,001- 8,000	83	85	+2	83	85	+2	84	86	+2
8,001-10,000	83	85	+2	84	86	+2	84	86	+2
10,001-20,000	86	87	+1	86	87	+1	86	88	+2
20,001+	84	86	+2	85	86	+1	85	87	+2
One-earner									
0- 2,000	94	95	+1	94	95	+1	94	95	+1
2,001- 2,500	94	95	+1	94	95	+1	95	95	0
2,501- 3,000	91	92	+1	91	92	+1	91	92	+1
3,001- 3,500	91	91	0	91	92	+1	91	92	+1
3,501- 4,000	89	90	+1	89	90	+1	89	90	+1
4,001- 5,000	90	90	0	90	91	+1	90	91	+1
5,001- 6,000	87	88	+1	87	89	+2	87	89	+2
6,001- 8,000	88	89	+1	89	89	0	88	89	+1
8,001-10,000	87	89	+2	88	89	+1	88	89	+1
10,001-20,000	89	90	+1	89	90	+1	89	90	+1
20,001+	90	91	+1	90	91	+1	90	91	+1

Appendix 3

Disaggregation of the 1937–1950 Reported Earnings Measure

To correctly calculate the lifetime earnings measure, the 1937–1950 summary taxable earnings measure had to be disaggregated into year-specific reported earnings measures. This was accomplished by using the year-specific estimated annual quarters of coverage from 1937 to 1950 and the 1937–1950 summary taxable earnings measure. The following procedure was employed to estimate the year-specific reported earnings for 1937 to 1950. First, the estimated reported earnings for year i ($EREP_i$) was calculated by

$$EREP_i = (EQC_i/TEQC)\, w_i \left(\sum_{i=1937}^{50} w_i/14 \right) (TOTAL50) \qquad \text{(A3.1)}$$

where EQC_i is estimated quarter of coverage in year i; TEQC is total estimated quarters of coverage from 1937 to 1950; w_i is average annual earnings for fulltime manufacturing employee in year i; $\sum_{i=1937}^{50} w_i/14$ is average annual earnings for fulltime manufacturing employee over the 1937–1950 time period; and TOTAL50 is total reported earnings for the 1937–1950 time period, as reported in the Longitudinal Exact Match File. Hence, the estimated reported earnings are divided over the time interval proportionally to the estimated annual quarters of coverage and average annual earnings in manufacturing from 1937 to 1950.

Because the estimated reported earnings measures were adjusted for the changes in average earnings over time, the sum of the estimated reported earnings measures will not, in all likelihood, equal the total reported earnings reported in the Longitudinal Exact Match File. The estimation error is

$$\text{BIAS} = \text{TOTAL50} - \sum_{i=1937}^{50} \text{EREP}. \qquad \text{(A3.2)}$$

The estimation error may be positive or negative depending on the location of the estimated quarters of coverage over the 1937–1950 time interval. The worker's estimated reported earnings are proportionally adjusted by the estimation error. That is, the estimation error is spread over the time period so as to preserve the proportion of estimated reported earnings in year i to the total estimated reported earnings from 1937 to 1950. The proportion of estimated reported earnings in year i (EREP_i) to the total estimated reported earnings from 1937 to 1950 is represented by

$$\text{PRO}_i = \text{EREP}_i / \sum_{i=1937}^{1950} \text{EREP}_i \qquad \text{(A3.3)}$$

for i = 1937 to 1950. The adjustment factor for each year (ADJ_i) is

$$\text{ADJ}_i = \text{PRO}_i \times \text{BIAS} \qquad \text{(A3.4)}$$

for i = 1937 to 1950. Finally, the adjustment factor for each year is used to adjust the estimated reported earnings for the same year. Hence, the reported earnings for year i (REP_i) is

$$\text{REP}_i = \text{EREP}_i + \text{ADJ}. \qquad \text{(A3.5)}$$

Notes

Introduction

1. Social Security is broadly defined as the federal Old-Age, Survivors, Disability, and Health Insurance (OASDHI) program. Prior to 1966, when the health insurance program was added, it was referred to as OASDI. This book confines its empirical analysis to the old-age (OAI) portion of OASDHI, which includes primary worker, spousal, transitional, and special age-72 benefits.
2. Parsons and Munro (1977) find that within the next 50 years the intergenerational transfer will disappear completely; hence, each retirement cohort will distribute among its members the amount of money they initially paid into the program. Similar results regarding the diminution of the intergenerational transfer were found by Freiden, Leimer, and Hoffman (1976) and Burkhauser and Warlick (1981). See chapter 2 for a more detailed discussion.
3. A common measure for assessing how a worker fares over a lifetime under the Social Security program is the (internal) rate of return on Social Security contributions. An (internal) rate of return is defined as the interest rate that equalizes the compounded value of accumulated payroll taxes paid over a worker's work history and the discounted present value of an expected stream of retirement benefits at the point of retirement.
4. Based on 1980 Social Security long-range cost projection assumptions, the real rate of return is expected to fall to 3 percent for the 2005 retirement cohort and to between 2 and 3 percent for subsequent retirement cohorts (Leimer and Petri, 1981). Ferrara and Lott (1985) calculated real rates of return ranging between −1.5 and 2.75 percent for 1983 labor-force entrants. Other studies summarized by Aaron (1982) estimated projected rates of return varying between 2.5 and 4 percent for workers entering the labor force between 1960 and 2000.
5. Stiglin (1981) argues that while certain groups of women (e.g., working married women) are subject to inequitable treatment under the Social Security program, women as a group are treated quite favorably when all advantages are weighed against the inequities. Advantages include women's longer life expectancies and the fact that virtually all spousal and survivor benefits are received by female beneficiaries (as opposed to male beneficiaries).
6. Working married women who qualify for insured worker benefits have survivorship and disability insurance protection not available to nonworking married women. Therefore, dependents benefits do not *fully* duplicate insured worker benefits.

7. Average indexed monthly earnings (AIME) is the basis for determining the primary insurance amount for workers who attain age 62 after 1978.

8. If the husband or wife dies, there is an even greater disparity in benefits between one-earner and two-earner couples with the same AIME. For example, if the husband in family A dies, his widow receives a widow benefit equal to $684. However, the surviving widow in family B would receive $479 in the event her husband dies. The widow in family B receives $205 less than the widow in family A (a 43-percent benefit advantage).

9. The same marriage duration requirement applies to surviving divorced wife benefits.

10. The earnings test applies to eligible beneficiaries aged 62 to 64, but the 1986 annual exempt amount is $5,760 per year.

11. This point is discussed in more detail in chapter 1.

12. In the 1983 amendments, the delayed retirement credit was increased to 3 percent per year for each year retirement is delayed past age 65. The credit ceases at age 70.

Chapter 1

1. This chapter provides a brief historical discussion of specific provisions of the old-age insurance program relevant to the distributional issue. For a more in-depth historical overview of the Social Security program, see Altmeyer (1963), Ball (1973), Myers (1985), and Witte (1963) for the views of those who helped to create the initial legislation and Achenbaum (1986), Derthick (1979), Ferrara (1980), and Light (1985) for the views of current Social Security scholars. For a general summary of all current OASDHI provisions and their historical development, see U.S. Social Security Administration (1985a and 1985b). Provisional changes introduced in the 1983 legislation are described in Svahn and Ross (1983) and Webster and Perry (1983).

2. Noncontributory, supplemental security benefits were not extended to husbands of female workers until 1950. In 1950, husband and widower benefits were extended to the husband of a female worker if he could prove that one-half of his support came from his working wife or deceased wife. The "dependency test" was stricken from the law after it was declared unconstitutional by the Supreme Court in 1977 (*Califano v. Goldfarb*).

3. Supplemental benefits were envisioned by the Advisory Council as a stop-gap adequacy provision. Over time, women were expected to enter the labor force and become eligible for their own retired worker benefits, resulting in the eventual phasing out of noncontributory, supplemental benefits. Lawmakers assumed: "Because most wives in the long run will build up wage credits on their own accounts as a result of their own employment these supplementary allowances will add but little to the ultimate cost of the system. They will, on the other hand, greatly increase adequacy . . . of the system by recognizing that the probable need of the married couple is greater than of a single individual" (Congressional Record, 1939).

4. There was a 20-fold increase from 1950 to 1971 in women receiving primary-worker benefits. Fifty percent of the female beneficiaries were receiving primary-worker benefits and 50 percent were claiming auxiliary benefits. The average monthly check for female beneficiaries was $100 (Bixby, 1972). According to the 1982 New Beneficiary Survey conducted by the Social Security Administration, 35 percent of married women

received benefits solely as wives on their husband's earnings record. The remaining 65 percent of married women collected benefits as primary workers; of these women, 25 percent were dually entitled (i.e., their primary benefit was supplemented by partial wife benefits), 27 percent received a retired-worker benefit only, and 13 percent received retired-worker benefits and also had husbands who were not yet retired (Social Security Administration, 1985c).

5. See Lampman and MacDonald (1982) for a discussion of the difference between an individualistic and familistic approach in defining the appropriate household unit for tax-transfer programs.

6. In 1940, 17 percent of married women were represented in the labor force compared to 55 percent in 1986. The labor force participation of women is expected to continue its upward trend in the future. The actuaries of the Social Security Administration project a labor force participation rate of approximately 67 percent in 1990 for women aged 25 to 54.

7. In 1984, only 6 percent of all families were made up of the traditional nuclear family in which the man works and the woman is a full-time homemaker. Overall, 90 percent of married women work in covered employment during their lifetime.

8. The "Ponzi-like" financing scheme is financially sound provided economic and population growth exceed growth in the size of the retirement population (Aaron, 1966; Pechman, Aaron, and Taussig, 1968; Samuelson, 1958). According to the Samuelson and Aaron overlapping-generation model, at least one generation can be made better off (with none worse off) by a "pay as you go" program provided the growth rate of population and per capita earnings exceed the real interest rate.

9. The AME is a summary measure of the worker's earnings history calculated by summing the total taxable earnings in the computation years divided by the number of months in the computation period. The AME measure was replaced by a wage-indexed base called the average indexed monthly earnings (AIME) in 1977. The AIME indexes the worker's earnings so that taxable earnings earned at different points in the life cycle are expressed in terms of the overall earnings levels prevailing in the year of eligibility. The PIA is the basis for all benefit payments and is a function of the worker's AME (or AIME after 1977).

10. For workers reaching age 62, dying, or becoming disabled in 1986, the formula is: 90 percent of the first $294 of AIME, plus 32 percent of the next $1,411 of AIME, plus 15 percent of the AIME remainder.

11. This point will be explored further in chapter 2.

12. In the 1983 amendments, Congress raised the retirement age, effective for workers who attain age 62 after year 2000. The new law raises the full benefit retirement age by 2 months per year from year 2000 to year 2005, inclusive, to age 66. Beginning in 2017, the retirement age will again rise by 2-month increments over a 6-year period for workers who turn age 62 in year 2017. The full benefit retirement age will be 67 for workers attaining age 62 after year 2021 (i.e., for those workers born after 1959). For more specific details, see U.S. Social Security Administration (1985b).

13. The actuarial assumptions underpinning the formulation of the adjustment factor are discussed in Myers (1963).

14. Future beneficiaries who retire at age 62 will receive checks reduced by 25 percent in 2005 and 30 percent in 2022.

15. In 1983, workers who postpone applying for retirement benefits receive benefits that are increased by 3 percent for each year acceptance is delayed past age 65 up to a maximum of 15 percent (age 70).

16. The loss in benefits may be partially or fully offset by the worker's higher PIA as a result of the worker's extended earnings history.

17. For a disputatious discussion of the delayed retirement credit on work incentives after age 62, see Blinder, Gordon, and Wise (1980 and 1981) and Burkhauser and Turner (1981).

18. Since 1973, benefits were reduced by $1 for every $2 of earnings above the earnings ceiling. Beginning 1 January 1986, worker-beneficiaries aged 65 to 70 lost $1 of benefits for every $2 of earnings over $7,800 ($650 per month), whereas younger retirees, aged 62 to 64, forfeited $1 of benefits for every $2 of earnings over $5,760 ($480 per month). Both earnings limits are automatically indexed to average wage increases. Beginning in 1990, beneficiaries aged 62 to 70 will lose $1 for every $3 of earnings over the annual earnings limit.

19. Beginning in 1983, the earnings test applies only to worker-beneficiaries who are aged 62 to 70.

20. The expansion of Social Security beginning in 1969 is described in Derthick (1979).

21. Benefits are adjusted annually if the CPI changes by 3 percent or more. If the CPI changes by less than 3 percent in a year, benefits will not be indexed until the cumulative change exceeds 3 percent. Under the 1983 law, cost-of-living adjustments (COLA) will be effective in December of each year. The (COLA) adjustment factor will be used on the lesser of the increase in prices (CPI) or average wages when the trust fund reserves fall to less than 15 percent (20 percent after 1988) of the expected year's benefit payment. If beneficiaries lose money because of this provision, a "catch-up" benefit will be paid when the combined trust fund balance reaches 32 percent of expected expenditures.

Chapter 2

1. Survivor probabilities measure the likelihood of an individual of life age x surviving to life age x+1.

2. The effect of socioeconomic factors on mortality is more pronounced for persons aged 25 to 64; however, the effect of these characteristics is still relevant, in most cases, at advanced ages (i.e., age 65 and older).

3. See Thompson (1983), pp. 1436–38.

4. The income-smoothing feature of the program focuses on the transfer of labor earnings from the worker's high-earnings years to her retirement years through the contribution-benefit mechanism of the program.

5. Brittain also calculated internal rates of return. Estimated real rates of return ranged from 2.78 to 6.28 percent.

6. Like Brittain, Chen and Chu computed internal rates of return. Rates of return for 1974 retirees varied between 6.1 and 16.9 percent. Rates of return for 22-year-old 1974 entrants were 1.4 to 8.5 percent. Yields between 1.1 and 7.7 percent were calculated for 18-year-old 1974 entrants.

7. The PIA is the amount payable to a retired worker who begins to receive retirement benefits at age 65.

8. It takes approximately 40 years for a retirement program to reach full maturity.

9. The AME is a summary measure of the worker's earnings history calculated by summing the total taxable earnings in the computation years divided by the number of months in the computation period. The PIA is a function of the worker's AME. The AME measure was replaced by a wage-indexed base called average indexed monthly earnings (AIME) in 1977.

Chapter 3

1. Total OAI contributions were also compounded using a bond rollover scheme. The bond rollover scheme assumed the government invested the full amount of the worker's annual OAI contributions into a government bond with the longest maturity that did not exceed the number of years from the date of investment to retirement. The coupon and principal were rolled over immediately upon maturity into the next longest bond that had a "correct" maturity period.

   Both compounding schemes rendered roughly identical total OAI contribution values. The mean difference between accumulated OAI contributions under the two compounding schemes was $300. The traditional compounding scheme rendered slightly larger total OAI contributions. Because of the small difference between the values generated by the different schemes, results will only be reported for the traditional compounding scheme. For a complete description of the bond rollover scheme, a complete historical table of market yields on U.S. government securities at constant maturity (1-, 3-, 5-, 10-, 20-, and 30-year) from 1937 to 1972, and for a comparison of the calculated traditional and rollover total OAI contribution values, see Wolff (1984).

2. For expository convenience, it is assumed in equation 3.3 that the husband and wife are the same age and retire at the same age. This assumption is dropped in chapter 4.

   The Z term captures the joint probability of the household surviving each successive month in the retirement period.

Chapter 4

1. It was sufficient to have one record in a married couple satisfy the above criteria to get both records included in the sample. Annuity calculations for married persons require the preservation of the family unit.

2. To be considered a "good match," all members of a stats unit must have matched Summary Earnings Record, Internal Revenue Service, and Master Beneficiary Record data present on the file as well as a certain level of agreement between demographic information.

3. Special age-72 benefits are monthly benefits payable to a person aged 72 (before 1972 for male and 1970 for female) or over without sufficient quarters of coverage to qualify for a retired-worker benefit under either the full or transitional insured-status provisions.

   Transitional benefits are monthly benefits payable to a person aged 72 (before 1969) who has at least one quarter coverage for every year after 1950 up to the year he/she reached age 65 (male) or 62 (female) with at least three quarters accumulated.

4. The shifting assumption is controversial (Brittain, 1971 and 1972a; Feldstein, 1972 and 1974; Hammermesh, 1979; MacRae and MacRae, 1976; Munnell, 1974; Vroman, 1974) but conventional in most studies of individual equity (Aaron, 1977; Brittain, 1972b;

Burkhauser and Warlick, 1981; Freiden, Leimer, and Hoffman, 1976; Hurd and Shoven, 1983; Leimer, 1978; Moffit, 1982; Okonkwo, 1976; Pellechio and Goodfellow, 1983). There are a few computer simulation studies, based on representative individual equity measures, that have attempted to isolate the effect of the shifting assumption in individual equity measures. For instance, Chen and Chu (1974) found that internal rates of return are negatively related and contribution-benefit ratios positively related to the degree of backward shifting, ceteris paribus.

5. The decomposition of OASDI rates is especially important when benefit comparisons are made across women with different labor-homemaker decisions. A working woman covered by Social Security is eligible for disability benefits, and her family is eligible for survivors benefits, on the basis of her OASDI contributions in the event she should become disabled or die prior to retirement. The nonworking woman and her family are not offered these benefits if the nonworking woman should become disabled or die. The nonworking woman is eligible for disability or survivorship benefits if the disability or death contingency occurs to her husband. Hence, the survivor and disability insurance coverage extended to the working woman prior to retirement are not duplicated by her husband's OASDI contribution.

6. A whole life annuity immediate pays the first payment one payment interval after the date of purchase and is purchased with a single premium. See Jordan (1975) for annuity formula derivations.

7. The assumption regarding expected growth in future price is based on the Social Security Trustee Report intermediate II-B projection on inflation for 1972 of 2.75 percent.

8. A joint-and-two-thirds annuity is comparable to purchasing a single annuity on each member's life and a joint-and-survivor annuity on both lives. The joint-and-two-thirds replicates the OAI program. It has an upper bound of one if both members survive, pays two-thirds if there is one survivor, and has a lower bound of zero if there are no survivors in the group.

9. The effective interest rate used to calculate an annuity that pays geometrically increasing payments is $i' = (i - c)/(1 + c)$ where i = the nonindexed interest rate and c = the future growth in prices.

10. For a recent discussion on the debate over Social Security and savings, see Lesnoy and Leimer (1986). The effect of Social Security on the labor supply is reviewed by Floersheim-Boaz (1986) and Thompson (1983).

Chapter 5

1. The earnings test operates to reduce the beneficiary's annuity benefit by 50 cents for every dollar of postretirement earnings greater than $1,680 but less than $2,280 and by one dollar for every dollar of earnings over $2,280 providing the beneficiary is younger than 72.

2. The magnitude of the program-type annuity benefit differential will diminish and its sign will eventually reverse over time because annuity benefits received from an indexed program are augmented by $(1 + c)^t$ and nonindexed benefits remain fixed in nominal terms.

3. Social Security Bulletin data show the average benefit for women workers to be about 60 percent higher than the wife's auxiliary (dependents) benefit for this time period.

4. Summary findings on annuity types 1, 2, 3, 4, and 5, male-to-female comparisons by annuity type, household-type comparisons by annuity type, and indexed-to-nonindexed comparisons by annuity type can be found in appendix 2, tables A2.1, A2.2, A2.3, A2.4, A2.5, and A2.6.
5. Recall that the Social Security program has two primary features: 1) an income-smoothing feature whereby workers transfer a fraction of their labor earnings to their retirement years by participating in the program during their earning years; and 2) an intergenerational transfer feature whereby income is transferred from the current working generation to the currently retired population.

Chapter 6

1. Loglinear and linear forms were also estimated; however, the quadratic form provided the best fit of the data.
2. Only household units in which both the husband and wife were retired in 1972 were included in the data set used to estimate model 6.2.
3. Loglinear and linear models were also estimated, but the reported model resulted in the best fit of the data.

Chapter 7

1. Ordinary least-squares (OLS) linear regression results are reported for all survivorship assumptions without education dummies by Meyer and Wolff (1987).
2. See Meyer and Wolff (1987) for OLS linear regression results for one-earner and two-earner couples.
3. These results were consistent across alternative model specifications—linear and log-linear regression models. Also, similar patterns were found for one-earner couples and two-earner couples when the married regression models were estimated separately for each married couple type.

Chapter 8

1. Two cautionary notes are required regarding direct comparisons between tabular and regression results. First, the tabular and regression results are derived from different groupings of the same retirement sample. Some of the tables (e.g., table 5.1) include all single workers and married couples where at least *one* member of the couple was retired in 1972. But the subsample used to derive regression results includes either single workers or married couples where *both* members were retired in 1972. Second, measures of income differ between the two analyses. Tabular results are arrayed by 1972 family income. Regression results are based on lifetime earnings, a summary statistic representing the accumulated value of annual taxable real earnings for the family unit. Tabular results are directly comparable with Burkhauser and Warlick's (1981) results. The lifetime income measure used in the regression analysis permits comparisons with Freiden, Leimer, and Hoffman (1976).
2. The scheduled increased in the delayed retirement credit is expected to equalize lifetime benefit streams for work after age 65. This change and the new "$1 for $3" earnings test withholding rate are expected to reduce the inequity between working and nonworking persons aged 65 to 70.

3. A similar principle of equity was proposed by Ozawa (1984).

4. Intracohort redistribution is not precluded by this definition of intergenerational equity.

5. Less popular family reform proposals include homemaker credits, double-decker reform, and two-tier reform. The homemaker credit plan is described by Holden (1982). See Warlick, Berry, and Garfinkel (1982) for a discussion of the double-decker proposal. Munnell and Stiglin (1982) discuss the two-tier plan.

6. For extensive discussions of the earnings sharing reform proposal, see Burkhauser (1982 and 1984), U.S. Social Security Administration (1985d), and Kaltenborn (1981).

7. See U.S. Social Security Administration (1985d) for a summary of the Earnings Sharing Implementation Study.

Bibliography

Aaron, Henry J. "The Social Insurance Paradox." *Canadian Journal of Political Science* 32(3) (August 1966): 371–74.

———. "Demographic Effects on the Equity of Social Security Benefits." In *The Economics of Public Services,* pp. 151–73. Edited by M.S. Feldstein and R.P. Inman. New York: Macmillan, 1977.

———. *Economic Effects of Social Security.* Washington, D.C.: The Brookings Institution, 1982.

Achenbaum, W. Andrew. *Social Security: Visions and Revisions.* Cambridge: Cambridge University Press, 1986.

Altmeyer, Arthur J. *The Formative Years of Social Security.* Madison: University of Wisconsin Press, 1963.

Antonovsky, Aaron. "Social Class, Life Expectancy and Overall Mortality." In *Patients, Physicians and Illness,* pp. 1–27. Edited by E. Gartly Jaco. New York: Free Press, 1972.

Aziz, Faye; Kilss, Beth; and Scheuren, Frederick. *1973 Current Population Survey—Administrative Record Exact Match File Codebook, Part I.* Studies from Interagency Data Linkages, Report No. 8. U.S. Department of Health, Education, and Welfare, Social Security Administration, HEW Publication No. (SSA) 79-11750, 1978.

Ball, Robert M. "Social Security Amendments of 1972: Summary and Legislative History." *Social Security Bulletin* 36 (March 1973): 3–25.

Bayo, Francisco. "Mortality of the Aged." *Transactions of the Society of Actuaries* 24 (March 1972): 1–24.

Bixby, Lenore E. "Women and Social Security in the United States." *Social Security Bulletin* 35 (September 1972): 3–11.

Blinder, Alan S.; Gordon, Roger H.; and Wise, Donald E. "Reconsidering the Work Disincentive Effects of Social Security." *National Tax Journal* 33(4) (December 1980): 431–42.

———. "Rhetoric and Reality in Social Security Analysis—A Rejoinder." *National Tax Journal* 34(4) (December 1981): 473–78.

Board of Governors of the Federal Reserve System. *Banking and Monetary Statistics, 1900–42.* Washington, D.C.: National Capital Press, 1943.

———. *Banking and Monetary Statistics, 1941–1970.* Washington, D.C.: Government Printing Office, 1976a.

———. *Annual Statistical Digest, 1971–1975.* Washington, D.C.: Government Printing Office, 1976b.

Boskin, Michael. "The Economics of Labor Supply." In *Income Maintenance and Labor Supply,* pp. 163–80. Edited by Glen Cain and Harold Watts. New York: Academic Press, 1973.

———. "Social Security and Retirement Decisions." *Economic Inquiry* 15 (January 1977): 1–15.

Brittain, John A. "The Incidence of Social Security Payroll Taxes." *American Economic Review* 61 (March 1971): 110–25.

———. *The Payroll Tax for Social Security.* Washington, D.C.: The Brookings Institute, 1972a.

———. "The Incidence of Social Security Payroll Taxes: Reply." *American Economic Review* 62 (September 1972b): 739–42.

Browning, Edgar K. "Labor Supply Distortions of Social Security." *Southern Economic Journal* 42 (October 1975): 243–52.

Burkhauser, Richard V. "Are Women Treated Fairly in Today's Social Security System?" *Gerontologist* 19 (1979): 242–49.

———. "The Early Acceptance of Social Security—An Asset Maximization Approach." *Industrial and Labor Relations Review* 33 (July 1980): 484–92.

———. "Earnings Sharing: Incremental and Fundamental Reform." In *A Challenge to Social Security: The Changing Roles of Women and Men in American Society,* pp. 73–91. Edited by R.V. Burkhauser and K.C. Holden. New York: Academic Press, 1982.

———. "Alternative Social Security Responses to the Changing Roles of Women and Men." In *Controlling the Cost of Social Security,* pp. 141–62. Edited by Colin D. Campbell. Lexington, Mass.: Lexington, 1984.

Burkhauser, Richard V., and Holden, Karen C., eds. *A Challenge to Social Security: The Changing Roles of Women and Men in American Society.* New York: Academic Press, 1982.

Burkhauser, Richard V., and Quinn, Joseph. "The Effect of Changes in Mandatory Retirement Rules on the Labor Supply of Older Workers." Vanderbilt University, Department of Economics Working Paper No. 81–W01, 1981.

Burkhauser, Richard V., and Turner, John A. "A Time Series Analysis of Social Security and Its Effect on the Market Work of Prime Age Men." *Journal of Political Economy* 86 (August 1978): 701–15.

———. "Can Twenty-Five Million Americans Be Wrong? A Response to Blinder, Gordon, and Wise." *National Tax Journal* 34(4) (December 1981): 467–72.

———. "Is the Social Security Payroll Tax a Tax?" Vanderbilt University Department of Economics and Business Administration, Working Paper No. 18–W20, 1983.

Burkhauser, Richard V., and Warlick, Jennifer L. "Disentangling the Annuity from the Redistributive Aspects of Social Security in the United States." *The Review of Income and Wealth* 27 (December 1981): 401–21.

Cain, Glen G. *Married Women in the Labor Force: An Economic Analysis.* Chicago: University of Chicago Press, 1966.

Campbell, Colin D., and Campbell, Rosemary G. "Cost-Benefit Ratios Under the Federal Old-Age Insurance Program." *Old Age Income Assurance,* Compendium of Papers on Problems and Policy Issues in the Public and Private Pension System, Part III: *Public Programs* 72–84. 90th Congress, 1st session. Washington, D.C.: Government Printing Office, 1967.

Campbell, Rita Ricardo. "The Problems of Fairness." In *Crisis in Social Security: Problems and Prospects,* pp. 125–45. Edited by M.J. Boskin. San Francisco: Institute for Contemporary Studies, 1977a.

———. *Social Security: Promise and Reality.* Stanford: Hoover Institution Press, 1977b.

Chen, Yung-Ping, and Chu, K.W. "Tax-Benefit Ratios and Rates of Return under OASI: 1974 Retirees and Entrants." *Journal of Risk and Insurance* 41 (June 1974): 189–206.

Congressional Record, 13 July 1939, Senate, p. 9012.

Danziger, Sheldon. "Income Redistribution and Social Security: Further Evidence." *Social Service Review* 51 (March 1977): 179–84.

Danziger, Sheldon, and Plotnick, Robert. "Demographic Change, Government Transfers and Income Distribution." *Monthly Labor Review* 100 (April 1975): 7–11.

Derthick, Martha. *Policymaking for Social Security.* Washington, D.C.: The Brookings Institute, 1979.

Feldstein, Martin S. "The Incidence of the Social Security Payroll Tax Comment." *American Economic Review* 62 (September 1972): 735–38.

————. "Social Security, Induced Retirement and Aggregate Capital Accumulation." *Journal of Political Economy* 82 (September/October 1974): 905–26.

Ferrara, Peter J. *Social Security: The Inherent Contradiction.* San Francisco: Cato Institute, 1980.

Ferrara, Peter J., and Lott, John R. "Rates of Return Promised by Social Security to Today's Young Workers." In *Social Security Prospects for Real Reform,* pp. 13–32. Edited by P.J. Ferrara. Washington, D.C.: Cato Institute, 1985.

Floersheim-Boaz, Rachel. "Labor Market Behavior of Older Workers Approaching Retirement: A Summary of Evidence from the 1970s." In *Social Security: A Critique of Radical Reform Proposals,* pp. 103–26. Edited by Charles W. Meyer. Lexington, Mass.: Lexington Books, 1987.

Freiden, Alan; Leimer, Dean; and Hoffman, Ronald. "Internal Rates of Return to Retired Worker-Only Beneficiaries Under Social Security, 1967–70." *Studies in Income Distribution No. 5* (October 1976). U.S. Department of Health, Education, and Welfare, Social Security Administration.

Freidman, Joseph, and Sjogren, Jane. "Assets of the Elderly as They Retire." *Social Security Bulletin* 44 (January 1981): 16–31.

Garfinkel, Irwin, and Masters, Stanley H. *Estimating the Labor Supply Effects of Income Maintenance Alternatives.* New York: Academic Press, 1977.

Gove, Walter R. "Sex, Marital Status, and Mortality." *American Journal of Sociology* 79 (July 1973): 45–67.

Hammermesh, Daniel S. "New Estimates of the Incidence of the Payroll Tax." *Southern Economics Journal* 45 (April 1979): 1208–17.

Holden, Karen C. "Spouse and Survivor Benefits: Distribution Among Aged Women." *Research on Aging* 1 (September 1979): 302–19.

————. "Supplemental OASI Benefits to Homemakers Through Current Spouse Benefits, a Homemaker Credit, and Child-Care Drop-Out Years." In *A Challenge to Social Security: The Changing Roles of Women and Men in American Society,* pp. 41–65. Edited by R.V. Burkhauser and K.C. Holden. New York: Academic Press, 1982.

Homer, Sidney. *A History of Interest Rates.* New Brunswick, N.J.: Rutgers University Press, 1963.

Hurd, Michael D., and Shoven, John B. "The Distributional Impact of Social Security." National Bureau of Economic Reports, Working Paper No. 1155, 1983.

Jordon, Chester Wallace, Jr. *Society of Actuaries' Textbook on Life Contingencies.* Chicago: The Society of Actuaries, 1975.

Kaltenborn, Sara H. "Social Security: A Proposal to Improve Equity and Adequacy for Women." *Journal of Legislation* 8 (1981): 250–61.

Kilss, Beth, and Scheuren, Frederick J. "The 1973 CPS-IRS-SSA Exact Match Study." *Social Security Bulletin* 41 (October 1978): 14–22.

Kitagawa, Evelyn M., and Hauser, Philip M. *Differential Mortality in the United States.* Cambridge: Harvard University Press, 1973.

Lampman, Robert J. *Ends and Means of Reducing Income Poverty.* New York: Academic Press, 1971.

Lampman, Robert J., and MacDonald, Maurice. "Concepts Underlying the Current Controversy About Women's Social Security Benefits." In *A Challenge to Social Security: The Changing Roles of Women and Men in American Society,* pp. 21–40. Edited by R.V. Burkhauser and K.C. Holden. New York: Academic Press, 1982.

Leimer, Dean R. "Identifying Historical OAI, SI, and DI Tax Rates Under Alternative Program Definitions." Washington, D.C.: Social Security Administration, February 1976.

________. "Projected Rates of Return to Future Social Security Retirees Under Alternative Benefit Structures." In *Policy Analysis with Social Security Research Files,* pp. 235–68. U.S. Department of Health, Education, and Welfare, Social Security Administration, Research Report No. 52, HEW Publication No. (SSA) 79-11808, 1978.

Leimer, Dean R., and Petri, Peter A. "Cohort-Specific Effects of Social Security Policy." *National Tax Journal* 34(1) (March 1981): 9–28.

Lesnoy, Selig D., and Leimer, Dean R. "Social Security and Private Saving: Theory and Historical Evidence." In *Social Security: A Critique of Radical Reform Proposals,* pp. 69–102. Edited by Charles W. Meyer. Lexington, Mass.: Lexington Books, 1987.

Light, Paul. *Artful Work: The Politics of Social Security Reform.* New York: Random House, 1985.

MacRae, C. Duncan, and MacRae, Elizabeth Chase. "Labor Supply and the Payroll Tax." *American Economic Review* 66 (June 1976): 408–9.

Metropolitan Life Insurance Company. "Socioeconomic Mortality Differentials." *Statistical Bulletin* (January 1975): 54–56.

Meyer, Charles W., and Wolff, Nancy L. "Intercohort and Intracohort Redistribution under Old Age Insurance: The 1962–72 Retirement Cohorts." *Public Finance Quarterly,* forthcoming 1987.

Moffit, Robert A. "Trends in Social Security Wealth." In *Economic Transfers in the United States,* pp. 327–58. Edited by Marilyn Moon. NBER Studies in Income and Wealth, 49. Chicago: University of Chicago Press, 1982.

Munnell, Alicia H. "The Impact of Social Security on Personal Savings." *National Tax Journal* 27 (December 1974): 553–67.

Munnell, Alicia H., and Stiglin, Laura E. "Women and a Two-Tier Social Security System." In *A Challenge to Social Security: The Changing Roles of Women and Men in American Society,* pp. 101–24. Edited by R.V. Burkhauser and K.C. Holden. New York: Academic Press, 1982.

Murray, Janet. "Homeownership and Financial Assets: Findings from the 1968 Survey of Aged." *Social Security Bulletin* 35 (August 1972): 3–23.

Myers, Robert J. "Actuarial Reduction Factors for Early-Retirement Benefits." *Intergenerational Review on Actuarial and Statistical Problems in Social Security* 9 (1963): 31–38.

________. "United States Life Tables for 1969–71." *Transactions of the Society of Actuaries* 28 (1976): 93–116.

________. *Social Security.* 3rd ed. Homewood, Ill.: Richard D. Irwin, 1985.

Myers, Robert J., and Bayo, Francisco. "Mortality of Workers Entitled to Old-Age Benefits Under OASDI." *Transactions of the Society of Actuaries* 27 (1965): 416–31.

National Center for Health Statistics. *Life Tables for 1959–61.* Washington, D.C.: Public Health Services, U.S. Department of Health, Education, and Welfare, 1964.

Okonkwo, Ubadigko. "Intragenerational Equity Under Social Security." Washington, D.C.: International Monetary Fund, March 1976.

Ozawa, Martha N. "Income Redistribution and Social Security." *Social Service Review* 50 (June 1976): 208–23.

————. "Social Security: Toward a More Equitable and Rational System." Center for the Study of American Business, Publication No. 52. St. Louis: Washington University, 1982.

————. "The 1983 Amendments to the Social Security Act: The Issue of Intergenerational Equity." *Social Work,* March–April 1984, pp. 131–37.

Parsons, Donald O., and Munro, Douglas R. "Intergenerational Transfers in Social Security." In *Crisis in Social Security: Problems and Prospects,* pp. 65–86. Edited by M.J. Boskin. San Francisco: Institute for Contemporary Studies, 1977.

Pechman, Joseph A.; Aaron, Henry J.; and Taussig, Michael K. *Social Security Perspectives for Reform.* Washington, D.C.: The Brookings Institute, 1968.

Pellechio, Anthony J. "Social Security and Retirement Behavior." Ph.D. dissertation. Department of Economics, Harvard University, 1978.

Pellechio, Anthony, and Goodfellow, Gordon. "Individual Gains and Losses from Social Security Before and After the 1983 Amendments." *Cato Journal* 3(2) (Fall 1983): 426–40.

Pindyck, Robert S., and Rubinfeld, Daniel. *Econometric Models and Economic Forecasts,* 2nd ed. New York: McGraw-Hill Book Co., 1981.

Samuelson, Paul A. "An Exact Consumption-Loan Model of Interest With or Without the Social Contrivance of Money." *Journal of Political Economy* 66 (December 1958): 467–82.

Scheuren, F.J., and Tyler, B. "Matched Current Population Survey and Social Security Data Bases." *Public Data Use* 3 (July 1975): 7–10.

Sherman, Sally R. "Assets on the Threshold of Retirement." *Social Security Bulletin* 36 (August 1973): 3–17.

Stiglin, Laura E. "A Classic Case of Overreaction: Women and Social Security." *New England Economic Review* (January/February 1981): 29–40.

Svahn, John A., and Ross, Mary. "Social Security Amendments of 1983: Legislative History and Summary of Provisions." *Social Security Bulletin* 46(7) (July 1983): 3–48.

Thompson, Lawrence H. "The Social Security Reform Debate." *Journal of Economic Literature* 21 (December 1983): 1425–67.

U.S. Bureau of the Census. *Historical Statistics of the United States Colonial Times to 1957.* Washington, D.C.: Government Printing Office, 1960.

U.S. Bureau of the Census. *Historical Statistics of the United States Colonial Times to 1970, Part 2.* Washington, D.C.: Government Printing Office, 1975.

U.S. Department of Health, Education, and Welfare. Social Security Administration. *Social Security Bulletin: Annual Statistical Supplement,* 1972. Washington, D.C.: Government Printing Office, 1973.

U.S. Department of Health, Education, and Welfare. Social Security Administration. *Social Security Handbook,* 5th ed., 1973. Washington, D.C.: Government Printing Office, 1974.

U.S. President. *Economic Report of the President.* Washington, D.C.: U.S. Government Printing Office, 1976.

U.S. Social Security Administration. *Social Security Handbook/1985.* Washington, D.C.: U.S. Government Printing Office, 1985a.

U.S. Social Security Administration. *Social Security Bulletin. 1984–85 Annual Statistical Bulletin,* 1985b.

U.S. Social Security Administration. "Women and Social Security." *Social Security Bulletin* 48(2) (February 1985c): 17–31.

U.S. Social Security Administration. "Report on the Earnings Sharing Implementation Study." *Social Security Bulletin* 48(3) (March 1985d): 31–41.

Vroman, Wayne. "Employer Payroll Taxes and Money Wage Behavior." *Applied Economics* 6 (September 1974): 189–204.

Warlick, Jennifer L.; Berry, David E.; and Garfinkel, Irwin. "The Double-Decker Alternative for Eliminating Dependency Under Social Security." In *A Challenge to Social Security: The Changing Roles of Women and Men in American Society,* pp. 131–60. Edited by R.V. Burkhauser and K.C. Holden. New York: Academic Press, 1982.

Webster, Bryce, and Perry, Robert L. *The Complete Social Security Handbook.* New York: Dodd and Mead, 1983.

Witte, Edwin E. *The Development of the Social Security Act.* Madison: University of Wisconsin Press, 1963.

Wolff, Nancy L. "The Distributional Impact of the Social Security Program, 1962–72." Ph.D. dissertation, Iowa State University, 1984.

Name Index

Subject Index